THE BOOK OF
EGGFREE CAKES

Readers interested in the subject matter of this book
are invited to contact:

ISKCON Reader Services
P. O. Box 730, Watford, WD25 8ZE, United Kingdom
Phone: +44 1923 857244
readerservices@pamho.net • www.iskcon.org.uk

The Bhaktivedanta Book Trust
Korsnäs Gård, 14792 Grödinge, Sweden
Phone: +46 8 53029800 • Fax: +46 8 53025062
info@bbt.se • www.bbt.se

www.bbt.se

www.krishna.com

ISBN 978-91-7149-387-3

Printed in China 2013

THE BOOK OF
EGGFREE CAKES

Cintia Stammers

three almonds

Eggfree cakes have a long tradition.
They were already available five thousand years ago
when Lord Krishna was present on Earth.

Contents

PREFACE   13

INTRODUCTION   15

EGGFREE CAKES   15

COOKING CAN BE AN ACT OF MEDITATION   16

A FEW PRACTICAL HINTS   16

NECESSARY EQUIPMENT   17

OPTIONAL EQUIPMENT   17

WEIGHTS AND VOLUMES   18

APPROXIMATE MEASURES   18

BRITISH AND AMERICAN TERMS   18

INGREDIENTS   19

CAKE MIXING METHODS   25

HOW TO BAKE THE CAKE   27

TROUBLESHOOTING   28

Sponge Cakes   31

BIRTHDAY CAKE 1   32

BIRTHDAY CAKE 2   34

ARIETTE'S CAKE   35

MOCK CHOCOLATE CAKE   36

CARAMEL CAKE   37

COFFEE AND WALNUT CAKE   38

MOCHA CAKE   39

ROYAL ORANGE CAKE   40

SHEPHERD'S CAKE   42

QUICK YOGHURT SPONGE   43

VELVET CAKE   44

GENOESE CAKE   45

GINGER SANDWICH CAKE   46

VEGAN SPONGE   47

SUGARFREE SPONGE CAKE 48
EKADASHI FRUIT CAKE 49
LEMON SPONGE 50
HONEY SPONGE 52
QUICK MIX SPONGE 54
EKADASHI SPONGE 56
CREAM SPONGE 57
PARTY SPONGE 58

Squares, Wedges and Slices 61

BROWNIES 62
BANANA CAKE 64
BANANA AND CHERRY CAKE 65
BUTTERSCOTCH CAKE 66
SPICY CARROT CAKE 67
COCONUT CAKE 68
POLENTA CAKE 70
GOKULA CAKE 71
KRISHNA CAKE 72
APPLE CAKE 73
GINGER SQUARES 74
MACROBIOTIC CAKE 76
SWEETCORN CAKE 77
ORIENTAL CAKE 78
LANCASHIRE PARKIN 79
RHUBARB CAKE 80
GIANT JAM SCONE 82
RAISIN CAKE 83
TOFU CAKE 84
HONEY SQUARES 85
APRICOT CAKE 86
ORANGE AND CAROB SQUARES 88
GINGERBREAD 89
SPICE SLICE 90
CARROT CAKE 91

OLD-FASHIONED CARROT CAKE   92
TAHINI SQUARES   94
DATE SQUARES   95
CHARIOTEER CAKE   96
BASLER LECKERLI   97
PEACH SQUARES   98

Fruit Loaves and Tea Breads   101

FOLAR   102
PEANUT BUTTER CAKE   104
WALNUT MALT LOAF   105
CHERRY CAKE   106
AFTERNOON TEA CAKE   107
TRADITIONAL PANETONE   108
ORANGE TEA BREAD   109
NUTMEG CAKE   110
FIG CAKE   111
QUICK FRUIT CAKE   112
MOLASSES FRUIT CAKE   113
APPLE CRUMBLE CAKE   114
CHERRY LOAF   115
APPLE AND DATE CAKE   116
MARBLE CAKE   117
HONEY CAKE   118
WALNUT CAKE   119
CHRISTMAS CAKE   120
PRUNE AND BRAZIL NUT CAKE   122
DATE AND WALNUT CAKE   123
EASTER SIMNEL CAKE   124
STOLLEN   126
TUTTI FRUTTI CAKE   128
SEED CAKE   129
BANANA AND WALNUT CAKE   130
POTATO CAKE   131
CONTINENTAL SWEET LOAF   132

BOILED CAKE 133
SAFFRON TEA BREAD 134
BRAZILIAN CAKE 135
BARA BRITH 136
HAZELNUT CAKE 137
BARM BRACK 138
APPLE AND BANANA CAKE 140
APPLE TEA BREAD 141
LEMON TEA BREAD 142

Gâteaux and Cheesecakes 145

GRANDDAD'S COCONUT CAKE 146
CASSATA CAKE 148
CHEESECAKE 1 149
CHEESECAKE 2 150
THREE-COLOUR CAKE 152
DELICACY CAKE 154
PINEAPPLE CAKE 155
BLACK FOREST GÂTEAU 156
GAURANGA CAKE 158
NRISIMHA CAKE 159
FRUIT GÂTEAU 160
ALMOND CREAM CAKE 162
MANGO GÂTEAU 163
SWISS ROLL 164
NEAPOLITAN CAKE 166
STRAWBERRY GÂTEAU 167
GRANDMOTHER'S FRIDGE CAKE 168
COCONUT BISCUITS 168
GERMAN APPLE CAKE 169
FRIDGE CAKE 170
TIRAMISÙ 171
MILLE SFOGLIE 172
EASY PUFF PASTRY 174

SACHERTORTE   174
APFELSTRUDEL   176
SWEDISH SOCKERKAKA   178
FRUIT SOCKERKAKA   179
TIGER CAKE   181
UPSIDE DOWN CAKE   182
EKADASHI COCONUT CAKE   183
APPLE PUDDING CAKE   185
RASPBERRY GÂTEAU   186

Puddings 189

CRAZY CAROB PUDDING   190
SPONGE PUDDING   191
APPLE RING   192
SWEETCORN PUDDING   193
CHRISTMAS PUDDING 1   194
CHRISTMAS PUDDING 2   195
PLUM PUDDING   196

Small Cakes 199

ROCK CAKES   200
SCONES   201
GULAB JAMUNS   202
MUFFINS   204
CASSAVA CAKES 205
MAIDS OF HONOUR   206
LEBKUCHEN   207
PANCAKES   208
GLUTEN-FREE CAROB CAKES   209
DOUGHNUTS   210
SCOTCH POTATO CAKES   211

Savoury Cakes   213

SPINACH ROLL   214
VEGETABLE CAKE   216
LAYERED VEGETABLE CAKE   218
PIZZA ROLL   219
CELERY BREAD   221
CHRISTMAS CHESTNUT ROLL   223
TOMATO AND BASIL CAKES   225

Everyday Icings and Fillings   227

FRUIT FILLING   228
FRUIT AND NUT FILLING 1   228
FRUIT AND NUT FILLING 2   228
SWEETCORN ICING   229
RICOTTA ICING   229
MIXED NUT FILLING   230
ADUKI BEAN FILLING   230
SEE-THROUGH ICING   232
CRÈME PÂTISSERIE, OR CONFECTIONER'S CUSTARD   232
SOFT CHEESE ICING   233
TOFU ICING   233

Icings and Fillings
for Special Occasions   235

BUTTER ICING   236
CHANTILLY CREAM   236
GANACHE 1   237
GANACHE 2   237
VEGAN CHANTILLY CREAM   238
CAROB ICING   238

CAROB FROSTING   239
LEMON ICING   239
ORANGE ICING   239
PEANUT BUTTER ICING   240
SHRIKHAND ICING   240
MOULDING ICING   242
MARZIPAN-ALMOND PASTE   242
VEGAN CREAM   243
MOCK CHOCOLATE 1   243
MOCK CHOCOLATE 2   244
GLACÉ ICING   244
FUDGE ICING   245

Adapting Recipes   247

HOW TO CHOOSE RECIPES   248
HOW TO ADAPT RECIPES   248
WHAT TO DO WHEN EVERYTHING'S GONE WRONG   249
TRUFFLES   249
TRIFLE   250
"CHINESE PUDDING"   250

Index   251

This book is dedicated to His Divine Grace
A.C. Bhaktivedanta Swami Prabhupada
Founder-Acharya of the International Society for Krishna Consciousness

Preface

Soon after meeting Hare Krishna devotees in 1974, I adopted their vegetarian diet and gave up all meat, fish and eggs. It did not take long for me to notice that I would not be able to eat or make cakes anymore, because practically all cakes are made with eggs. At the time I lived in Sao Paulo, Brazil, and at the temple there, no one knew how to make cakes without eggs.

Little by little the devotees and I started to experiment with locally available ingredients. Although in the beginning some of the experiments were rather frustrating because the cakes came out either too hard or too stodgy, we soon came up with some good recipes. At home my attempts sometimes went awry, and the ducks in the pond nearby certainly ate more cake than I. But there were some good results too, and the list of eggfree cakes started to grow.

In 1975 and 1976 I had the chance to visit several temples in the United States and Europe and, of course, to collect recipes from cooks everywhere. When I came to England in 1978, I found that it was easy to adapt many of the English and Scottish fruit cakes because the few eggs they require are easily replaced with other ingredients. Later, when I was homebound with two small children, I studied nutrition and had time to both experiment with the recipes I had already gathered and play with traditional recipes. Soon the recipes took on a new importance: how could I hold my children's birthday parties without cake?

It has taken a few years to collect the recipes into a book, but at last the time has come to share them with other cooks. Special thanks to Sadanandarupa, Mahamani and Sadbhuja for test-baking the cakes, to Janakarshi for taking the photos, to Govinda and Brahma Muhurta for designing the book, to Kshama for proofreading it, to Govinda Madhava for looking after the production and to my mother for her encouragement.

Hare Krishna!
Cintia Stammers

Introduction

Eggfree Cakes

The recipes in this book will be especially useful to two groups of people: vegetarians of all sorts and people allergic to eggs. From a nutritionist's point of view, an eggfree cake with low sugar and fat content offers the following:

* iron (from wheat flour)
* calcium (from milk and yoghurt)
* protein (from milk, nuts, soya milk and yoghurt)
* vitamin A (from milk and butter)
* vitamin D (from milk, butter and vegetable margarine)

One of the advantages of eggfree cakes is their low cholesterol level. It goes without saying that the use of butter and cream needs to be restricted to special occasions.

Some people are allergic to lactose, the sugar present in milk. For them, it is recommended that they replace the milk in the recipes with soya milk. The recipes in this book do not use chocolate or cocoa. Chocolate contains stimulants, which makes it both addictive and generally bad for one's health. Besides, because it is a naturally bitter product, large amounts of sugar are needed to make it taste pleasant. It is replaced by carob and vanilla.

Every cake needs sugar, not only for flavour but for consistency. Sugar is an essential element in the chemical process that the cake mixture goes through when heated in the oven. A cake without sugar will not rise, nor will it have the right consistency. These recipes require only the minimum amount of unrefined sugar necessary to give the cake the right consistency. A few recipes do not require any sugar, using fruit sugar or dried fruit instead. These recipes are ideal for diabetics.

For those people who worry about calories or cholesterol, recipes which use sunflower oil are recommended. These contain less fat than those using margarine or butter.

Cooking Can Be an Act of Meditation

The Vedic scriptures explain that we can offer Krishna vegetables, fruit, cereals and milk products. The recipes in this book are based on this precept. The act of offering and sharing food – prasada – is an act of meditation, and it is simple. Eating only food offered to Krishna is the perfection of vegetarianism.

While shopping, we should be aware that we may find meat, fish and egg products mixed with other foods; so we should make sure to read labels carefully. For instance, some brands of yoghurt and sour cream contain gelatin, a substance made from the horns, hooves and bones of slaughtered animals. Nor can we offer Krishna coffee or tea that contain caffeine. Those who like these beverages can purchase caffeine-free coffee and herbal teas.

We should not taste any of the preparations while cooking them or before offering them to Krishna. We must also make sure that the kitchen, we ourselves and the utensils being used are clean. We should not eat or drink while preparing food.

When the cake is ready, place it in front of a picture of Krishna. Use special dinnerware kept solely for this purpose. No one but the Lord should eat from those dishes. Then offer a simple prayer based on some of God's names: Hare Krishna, Hare Krishna, Krishna Krishna, Hare Hare/ Hare Rama, Hare Rama, Rama Rama, Hare Hare. This prayer should be recited three times.

Remember that the real purpose of preparing and offering food to the Lord is to show our devotion and gratitude to Him. Krishna accepts our devotion, not the physical offering itself. God is complete in Himself – He doesn't need anything. Out of His immense kindness, He allows us to offer food to Him so that we can develop our love for Him.

A Few Practical Hints

Each recipe contains the following information:

❀ Vegan: Recipes marked "vegan" contain ingredients which are of 100% vegetable origin.
❀ The list of ingredients needed for the recipe.
❀ Method: Indicates how the cake should be mixed.
❀ Cake tins: The type and size of cake tin and how it should be prepared.
❀ Oven temperature. Never place an unbaked cake in a cold oven. Always switch the oven to the correct temperature before starting to prepare the cake mixture.

❀ Baking time: the time necessary for the cake to bake from the minute it is placed in a hot oven.

Some recipes may also present:

❀ Variations: how recipes can be adapted so that flavours can be changed.

❀ Filling and icing ideas: ideas and suggestions for fillings and/or icings which best suit the cake. Capitalized expressions can be found in the two chapters entitled "Everyday Icings and Fillings" and "Icings and Fillings for Special Occasions".

Necessary Equipment

❀ a large mixing bowl
❀ a smaller bowl
❀ a large spoon for mixing
❀ teaspoons (5 ml) and tablespoons (15 ml) to measure the ingredients
❀ an old-fashioned wire egg whisk
❀ a measuring jug
❀ a sieve
❀ cake tins of varying sizes
The most commonly used are:
  • sponge or sandwich tins (round, flat tins): 18 cm (7") or 20 cm (8") in diameter
  • round, deep cake tin: 18 cm (7") or 20 cm (8") in diameter
  • rectangular tin or Swiss roll tin, about 20 × 30 cm (8" × 12")
    or 18 × 25 cm (7" × 10")
  • loaf tin: 500 g (1 lb) or 1 kg (2 lb)
  • fairy cake/muffin tin

Optional Equipment

❀ kitchen scales
❀ a plastic spatula
❀ a metal spatula knife to spread icings and fillings
❀ an electric mixer
❀ a blender or liquidizer and a nut grinder
❀ a rack on which to cool cakes that have just come out of the oven
❀ other cake tins of different sizes and shapes, such as a ring cake tin (round, with a hole in the centre) of about 18–20 cm (7"–8") in diameter

Weights and Volumes

1 cup = 240 ml = 8 fl oz
1 tablespoon = 15 ml = ½ fl oz
1 teaspoon = 5 ml = ⅙ fl oz

In the recipes, measurements are listed in both metric and imperial units, e.g. 200 g
(7 oz/1½ cups). When using metric or imperial measurements, it is advisable to use one or the
other; avoid mixing the two. Below is a list showing some examples of equivalent measurements.

Approximate Measures

100 g	(3½ oz/1 cup)	bread crumbs
120 g	(4 oz/½ cup)	butter, vegetable margarine
15 g	(½ oz/1 tablespoon)	butter, vegetable margarine
100 g	(3½ oz/1 cup)	carob powder
100 g	(3½ oz/1 cup)	coconut, desiccated
100 g	(3½ oz/1 cup)	cornflour
15 g	(½ oz/2 tablespoons)	cornflour
100 g	(3½ oz/1 cup)	flaked oats
100 g	(3½ oz/¾ cup)	flour
100 g	(3½ oz/½ cup)	maize flour/polenta
100 g	(3½ oz/½ cup)	nuts, chopped
100 g	(3½ oz/¾ cup)	raisins, sultanas, currants
100 g	(3⅔ oz/⅔ cup)	sugar: soft brown
100 g	(3½ oz/½ cup)	sugar: caster/muscovado

British and American Terms

[British — American]
cake tin — cake pan
caster sugar — superfine sugar
maize flour or polenta flour — cornmeal

cornflour — cornstarch
double cream — heavy cream
fairy cakes — cupcakes
golden unrefined sugar — turbinado sugar
greaseproof paper — baking parchment
icing sugar — confectioner's sugar
mixed peel — candied peel
mixed spice — apple pie spice
muscovado sugar — raw sugar
ring tin — tube or Bundt pan
sandwich cake — layer cake
sandwich sponge tin — layer cake pan
Swiss roll tin — jelly roll pan

Ingredients

Always use clean, dry spoons and cups when measuring ingredients. If using scales, make sure that the measuring dish is also clean and dry.

Wheat Flour

The most important ingredient in a cake is flour. Most recipes call for wheat flour, but some recipes call for maize, rice, buckwheat or potato flour. Try substituting half the amount of flour called for with wholemeal flour, either self-raising or plain, according to the recipe.

Wholemeal flour is rich in iron, calcium, sodium, potassium and magnesium as well as other minerals and vitamins that are lost when flour is refined. Always sift wholemeal flour first. You can use the bran left in the sieve for other dishes such as soups, cereal, etc.

Wholemeal flour may sometimes give cakes a denser or heavier consistency, but it will give a much better flavour. If using plain flour, make sure it is unbleached.

Self-raising flour — Sift together flour and baking powder in this proportion: 1 teaspoon baking powder to each 100 g (3 oz/1 cup) plain flour or equal amounts of plain and wholemeal flour. Mix the ingredients thoroughly and sieve them two or three times. Store in an airtight container, in a cool, dry place.

Other Flours

❋ Rice flour (also called ground rice): Because it is gluten-free, rice flour is recommended for babies, toddlers and people allergic to wheat.

❋ Potato flour: This is actually the starch found in potatoes. Use it with moderation because it can make the cake very dry.

❋ Cornflour (also called cornstarch): It gives sponges a light texture. Mixed with water, it can be used as a binder. Not all cornflour comes from maize, so if you are allergic to wheat, make sure that the type you buy is wheat-free.

❋ Buckwheat flour: Although slightly heavier than wheat flour, this is a wonderful flour for anyone who needs to avoid grains. It is darker in colour than wholewheat, and it is ideal for carob cakes.

❋ Arrowroot: This product comes from the root of the tropical plant aru. It can be used instead of cornflour as a binder. Sauces thickened with arrowroot retain their transparency, making it ideal for fruit juice icings.

❋ Carob powder: Carob powder or carob flour comes from the pod and seeds of the Mediterranean carob tree (*Ceratonia siliqua*). Both the seeds and the pulp around them are edible, and both are used in cooking.

Cocoa or chocolate contain stimulants (theobromine and caffeine), oxalic acid (which lowers the level of calcium in our bodies) and other toxins, such as phenyletilamine and tiramine (which may cause migraine headaches), and should therefore be avoided. The recipes used in this book always call for carob powder. If you are adapting recipes from other sources and are substituting carob for cocoa, remember to use less sugar, since carob is naturally sweeter than cocoa.

Baking Powder

Baking powder, a mixture of acids and alkali, works by reacting with the liquid in the mixture, which in turn produces carbon dioxide. When heated, the reaction speeds up, the bubbles expand and the cake rises. This rising effect, however, is lost with time, so cakes should be baked as soon as the baking powder has been added. If this is not possible – for example when making several batches – keep the mixture in the refrigerator.

Always use ingredients at room temperature. When making a cake using the melting method, leave the mixture to cool to almost room temperature before adding the flour and baking powder.

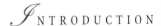

Raising agents should always be measured carefully. Used in excess, baking powder can cause the cake to rise too much and too violently, only to collapse when it comes out of the oven. If too little powder is used, the cake will not rise, impairing the texture and taste. It is possible to make your own baking powder at home:

50 g (2 oz/2 tablespoons) cream of tartar
25 g (1 oz/1 tablespoon) bicarbonate of soda
25 g (1 oz/1 tablespoon) fine rice flour or cornflour

Mix the three ingredients thoroughly and sieve them two or three times. Store the baking powder in an airtight tin or jar, in a cool, dry place.

Bicarbonate of Soda, Sodium Bicarbonate or Baking Soda

An alkali, bicarbonate of soda on its own is used in recipes which call for acid ingredients, such as lemon juice or sour milk. It gives cakes a darker colour. Because its taste is rather strong, it must be measured carefully and used with caution. Too much can make the cake taste of soap.

Yeast

Active yeast, both fresh and dried, is used in fruit breads and some cakes. The amount of fresh yeast used is approximately 15 g (½ oz) for each 500 g (1 lb) flour for ordinary dough, and 30 g (1 oz) for enriched dough. When using fresh yeast, buy it in small amounts and use within three days. Keep it stored in the refrigerator. Follow the manufacturer's instructions for using the various types of dried yeast.

Sugar

Cakes need sugar. However, recipes in this book call for the minimum amount of sugar necessary to give the cake the right texture. Sugar is an empty food and a main contributing factor to obesity, which in turn can cause heart disease. Sugar is also linked with diabetes and dental decay. Excess sugar is bad for everybody.

There is little difference between the damage done by white, refined sugar or brown sugar. Muscovado, or raw cane sugar, has small amounts of minerals. However, from the point of view of nutrition, this will make little difference to one's diet. On the other hand, molasses is a good source of iron. Below are the main types of sugar used in the recipes:

❊ Caster sugar or superfine sugar: Use unrefined golden (turbinado) caster sugar rather than white sugar, as the latter may contain bleaching agents. It is possible to grind your own sugar at home from ordinary unrefined sugar in a coffee or nut grinder.

❊ Muscovado sugar or raw sugar: True Muscovado sugar is lumpy and has the delicious taste of cane juice. Make sure that you are not sold refined sugar dyed with caramel colouring. Always dissolve it in the liquid in the recipe before adding it to the mixture.

❊ Soft brown sugar: This is a moist sugar, similar to Muscovado but with a lighter colour. Make sure that you buy unrefined sugar and not the refined, dyed variety.

❊ Honey: Some people do not cook with honey because it loses its minerals and vitamins and may even become slightly toxic if boiled. If you prefer, use molasses instead of honey when baking, and use honey for glazing baked cakes.

❊ Molasses: This is the unpurified residue from the process of crystallising sugar. It contains some minerals. Treacle, which is the first product from the refining of sugar and is also rich in iron, can be used instead.

❊ Golden syrup: Although it may give cakes a lovely golden colour, this is a product to be avoided as it is made from refined white sugar and is just as empty a food.

❊ Liquid glucose: This is also made of refined sugar and should be used with moderation – usually only for moulding icing.

❊ Icing sugar or confectioner's sugar: This is the most refined of sugars. Use it with caution for special occasions only. Better still, make your own by grinding unrefined golden sugar in a grinder. Grind one tablespoon at a time and sift it before using it in icings.

❊ Malt extract: This is a sugar derived from barley. It is wonderful for fruitcakes and malt loaves.

❊ Fructose: Even though this is a refined sugar, it is less harmful than white cane or beet sugar. Use it instead of caster sugar, but reduce the amount by one quarter.

❊ Maple syrup: This is a delicacy rather than a sugar, and it is very expensive. Use it for glazing plain cakes.

Fat

Fat helps to keep cakes moist and fresh. However, in excess, fat is bad for one's health and should therefore be used as little as possible.

❊ Butter: Use unsalted butter in icings and fillings. Butter can give cakes a heavy consistency, so use a combination of butter and soft vegetable margarine. Both should be softened to room temperature before using.

❋ Vegetable margarine: Use one that is low in hydrogenated vegetable oils. It can be used instead of butter.

❋ Sunflower oil: Sunflower oil is the best kind of fat for cakes without eggs. Although other vegetable oils can be used, they may lend cakes their particular flavours.

❋ Vegetable suet: This is nothing but shredded vegetable cooking fat tossed in rice flour or cornflour. You can make your own by grating hard, cold vegetable fat. Use it straight away or it will cling together again. This is the ingredient that gives steamed puddings their characteristic moisture and texture. It does not melt or mix with other ingredients during the mixing stage, but melts and penetrates everything once heated.

Liquid Ingredients

❋ Milk: Cow's milk can be substituted by any plant milk such as soya, almond, oats or rice.

❋ Cream: Use fresh whipping or double cream, always in moderation, and only for special occasions.

❋ Sour milk or soured milk: On warm days, if milk is kept out of the refrigerator, it will sour naturally in a few hours. If you want to make the milk curdle quickly, add the juice of a small lemon to ¼ litre (½ pint /1 cup) milk. The milk will curdle naturally and will be ready for use in about 20–30 minutes.

❋ Yoghurt: Use plain yoghurt or soya yoghurt.

❋ Condensed milk: This is another ingredient which must be used only for special occasions because of the high amount of refined sugar it contains.

❋ Fruit juice: Use orange or apple juice. Remember that certain fruit juices, such as pineapple or grapefruit, will strongly flavour the cake.

Dried Fruit and Nuts

Use raisins, pitted prunes, dried apricots, figs, apples, bananas, dates or whatever you can find where you live. If you buy fruit in bulk and unwrapped, remember to wash and dry it before adding it to a recipe. Cakes which use a large quantity of dried fruit take a long time to bake. If you want to shorten the baking time, boil the fruit in a little water before you prepare the mixture. Let it cool, drain it, and then add it to the recipe.

If you are using tinned fruit for decoration or for fillings, choose the variety which is preserved in fruit juice rather than in syrup.

Shell all nuts before weighing them. Many nuts can be used raw: almonds, Brazil nuts, pistachio nuts, walnuts, pecan nuts, cashew nuts, hazelnuts, sunflower seeds. However, the taste of some nuts, such as hazelnuts and almonds, is much improved by roasting. If using peanuts, roast them first.

Essences and Other Flavourings

❀ Essences: Avoid using artificial flavourings. Instead, try buying natural essences such as vanilla, almond or mint.

❀ Vanilla: It is easy to make vanilla sugar. Place a vanilla pod with the sugar in an airtight container and leave it for a few weeks before using it.

❀ Lemon and orange rind: If the recipe calls for grated lemon or orange rind, use unwaxed fruit. Wash and dry the fruit well before grating its skin.

❀ Spices: Several fruitcakes call for spices such as ginger, cinnamon, cloves, allspice, cardamom and nutmeg. It is a good idea to have small quantities of these spices at home. If they are stored in jars in a dry place, they keep their flavour for years. Mixed spice is a combination of ground cinnamon, ginger, allspice, nutmeg and cloves and can be bought ready mixed. Below is a basic recipe in case you prefer to mix your own.

Mixed Spice

Mix and sift together the following ground spices in this proportion and keep the mixture in an airtight jar:

1 tablespoon cinnamon
½ tablespoon ginger
1 teaspoon cardamom
1 teaspoon cloves
1 teaspoon nutmeg
1 teaspoon allspice
1 teaspoon dill seeds (optional)

Other Ingredients

❀ Cheese, including hard cheeses, cream cheeses, ricotta: always use cheeses made with vegetable rennet.
❀ Tofu, or soya curd cheese: use it grated or minced.
❀ Tahini: This is a paste made from sesame seeds. Although rich in minerals, it has a high fat content; therefore, use it in moderation.

Cake Mixing Methods

Each recipe states how the cake should be mixed. The summary below shows six basic methods, from the simplest to the more complicated. The instructions which follow should give you an idea of how these methods work. In the recipe section of the book, more detailed instructions will be given.

One-step Method

Sift the flour and the baking powder in a mixing bowl. Add the sugar and all other ingredients. Mix well with a spoon until thoroughly blended. The mixture will have a thick consistency and be light and glossy. It can be poured or spooned into the tin.

Dry and Wet Method

Many eggfree cakes are mixed this way. This is a simple, easy method and the least time-consuming. First weigh all dry ingredients into a bowl. In a measuring jug, measure and blend the liquid ingredients. Now combine both dry and wet mixtures. Beat for one minute and spoon or pour the mixture into the tin. If you are using caster sugar, add it to the flour. However, if you are using muscovado or soft brown sugar, dissolve it in the liquid.

Melting Method

This is an ideal method for honey, molasses or syrup cakes. Place the butter or margarine in a saucepan over low heat. When the fat has melted, remove the saucepan from the heat and add the honey, molasses, etc. Mix until well blended. Let it cool and then mix in the milk or other liquid and sugar. Carefully fold in the flour, baking powder and other ingredients.

Rub-in Method

Sift the flour and the baking powder into a mixing bowl. Chop the cold butter or margarine and rub it into the flour until the mixture resembles fine breadcrumbs. Blend in the liquid and sugar. The mixture will be thick and smooth and should be free from lumps.

Creaming Method

This is the most time-consuming method. Keep it for special occasions unless you enjoy beating, creaming, folding, etc.

Beat the softened butter or margarine with the caster or soft brown sugar until the mixture is light and fluffy. This can take more than five minutes by hand. Add the milk or other liquid a little at a time, stirring continuously. If the mixture curdles, stir in a little flour and then continue to add the liquid. Fold in the flour, a little at a time, stirring slowly. This mixture will be thick and creamy and have an opaque look. It can be poured or spooned into the tin.

Bread-making Method

Heat the water, milk or whey to about 40°C (100°F), until it is just warm to the finger. Pour it into a bowl and mix in the fresh yeast. If using dried yeast, follow the manufacturer's instructions. Add a tablespoonful of plain flour and mix well with a fork or whisk. Cover with a tea towel and set aside for ten minutes, until bubbles appear on the surface.

Gradually, add the rest of the flour, the salt and oil. Mix well with a spoon and then with your fingers. Alternatively, blend the flour and salt and pour the yeast mixture and oil over this dry mixture.

Sprinkle some flour over a wooden or stone working surface and place the mixture onto it. Knead for about ten minutes. If you prefer, divide the dough into several balls the size of a large orange and knead them one at a time for one minute. Combine all the bits together and form one large ball of dough. Place it in an oiled mixing bowl, cover with a clean tea towel, and leave it to prove for at least one hour. Knead the dough again for one minute and follow the recipe.

How to Bake the Cake

Preparing the Cake Tin

Before you start mixing the cake, prepare the baking tin or tins and turn the oven on to the right temperature. If you do not have the specific size tin, use your common sense and do not be afraid to adapt what is available.

The tin should be clean and dry and at room temperature. Avoid pouring the mixture into a hot tin. Grease the sides and bottom of the tin with butter or margarine and sprinkle with flour. Shake off the excess flour. For fruitcakes, grease the tin and line it with greaseproof paper. After baking, leave the cake to cool for about five or ten minutes before removing the paper. Don't leave it any longer or the paper may stick to the cake.

Shortcuts

If you are going to buy tins, buy the nonstick kind. Measure the bottom of the tin and cut several rounds of greaseproof paper the same size. When baking a cake, dab the bottom of the tin with butter or margarine and place the paper circle on it. Peel off the paper as soon as you have turned the cake onto a wire rack to cool.

Preparing the Oven

The cake mixture should be baked as soon as it is ready. If that is not possible, refrigerate the mixture until it can be baked. Always place the cake in the centre of the oven. If using a fan oven, the cake can be placed on any shelf, but never too near any one of the walls.

The cake mixture should always be placed into a hot oven. Once the cake is in the oven, do not open the oven door for at least ten minutes. Cold air can sometimes prevent the cake from rising properly.

Testing the Cake

Test to see if the cake is ready by inserting a skewer or cocktail stick into the centre of the cake. When it is ready, the skewer should come out clean and dry. If it doesn't, leave the cake in the oven for another five minutes and then try again.

Cooling the Cake

After removing the cake from the oven, let it stand for about five to ten minutes, or a little longer for fruit cakes, on a wire rack or grill, so that the bottom of the cake is also allowed to cool. Then turn the cake onto the rack, remove the tin and paper, if used, and leave it to cool.

Storing the Cake

Always store cakes in a dry, cool place. Sponge cakes can be stored for two to three days. Heavily iced cakes and gâteaux can be stored in the refrigerator for up to two days.

Rub-in cakes are best eaten on the same day. Some fruit cakes and malt loaves should be stored for a couple of days before serving, as their flavour improves with time. Rich fruit cakes can be stored for two to three weeks in an airtight tin.

Freezing the Cake

Sponges, sandwich and plain cakes can be wrapped in plastic wrap and frozen for up to two months. Iced cakes should be open frozen and then wrapped, but it is best to avoid freezing them altogether. Instead, freeze the cake and prepare the icing when it is needed.

Troubleshooting

In general, eggfree cakes are easier to make than cakes with eggs. However, sometimes cakes may go wrong. On the following page are some ideas of what may have gone wrong. Examine the cake, look at the list, and better luck next time!

Appearance:	Possible Causes:
Sunken cake	– too much liquid used – too much baking powder – too much butter or margarine
Cake looks and feels uncooked	– too little baking powder – stale baking powder – cake was taken out of the oven too soon – oven temperature too low
Heavy cake	– too little baking powder – too much butter, oil or margarine – too much liquid – stale baking powder
Dry cake	– too much baking powder – not enough oil or butter – cake kept in the oven for too long
Crumbly cake	– too much sugar – too much liquid – not enough binding ingredients, e.g. cornflour, vegetable oil
Cracked top	– oven too hot – cake tin too small – not enough liquid in the mixture
Uneven surface	– oven shelf is uneven – oven may be heating up unevenly – cake was placed too near one of the sides of the oven

SPONGE CAKES

These recipes prove that it is possible to make soft, moist and tasty cakes without using eggs. The cakes should have a consistency similar to that of cakes sold by professional bakers.

Most cakes in this section call for some form of filling, and some are also iced. Choose your favourite filling or icing from the ideas below each recipe.

Traditionally, these cakes are baked in two round, shallow tins, called sandwich or sponge tins, of the same size. However, they can also be baked in a deep cake tin and, when cold, halved horizontally and filled.

Birthday Cake 1

VEGAN

100 ml (3½ fl oz/½ cup) sunflower oil
½ teaspoon vanilla essence
150 g (5 oz/¾ cup) caster sugar
100 ml (3½ fl oz/½ cup) yoghurt or soya yoghurt
300 g (10 oz/2½ cups) plain flour
5 teaspoons baking powder
200 ml (7 fl oz/¾ cup) milk or soya milk

❀ Creaming method
❀ Cake tins: two 25 cm (10") round sandwich tins or one deep
   25 cm (10") round tin, greased and floured
❀ Oven temperature: 190°C (375°F/Gas Mark 5)
❀ Baking time: 25 minutes

Cream together the oil, vanilla, sugar and yoghurt. Sift the flour and the baking powder over the mixture. Gradually add the milk and beat for 1 minute with a spoon.

Turn the mixture into the prepared tins. Bake for 25 minutes. Using a skewer, check if the centre of the cake is dry. If it is not, leave in the oven for another 5 minutes.

Remove from the oven and allow to cool for 10 minutes. Turn out onto a wire cooling rack. Let it cool completely before filling and icing.

Filling and icing ideas: Chantilly Cream, Vegan Chantilly Cream, Butter Icing, Ganache.

Birthday Cake 2

200 g (7 oz/1½ cups) flour
100 g (3½ oz/½ cup) caster sugar
4 teaspoons baking powder
¼ teaspoon bicarbonate of soda
50 g (2 oz/½ cup) carob powder
100 ml (3½ fl oz /½ cup) milk
4 tablespoons condensed milk
60 g (2 oz/¼ cup) melted butter
½ teaspoon vanilla essence
50 ml (2 fl oz/¼ cup) warm water

❀ One-step method
❀ Cake tins: two 20 cm (8") round tins, greased and floured
❀ Oven temperature: 180°C (350°F/Gas Mark 4)
❀ Baking time: 25–30 minutes

In a bowl, sift the flour, sugar, baking powder, bicarbonate of soda and carob powder. Add the milk, condensed milk, melted butter, vanilla and water. Beat with a spoon for two minutes.

Spoon the mixture into the prepared tins. Bake for 25 minutes. Check if the centre of the cake is dry. If it is not, leave in the oven for another 5 minutes. Remove from the oven and allow to cool for 10 minutes. Turn out onto a wire cooling rack. Let it cool completely before filling and icing.

Filling and icing ideas: Chantilly Cream, Crème Pâtisserie (chocolate flavour), Ganache, Shrikhand Icing.

Ariette's Cake

VEGAN

the juice of 1 lemon
200 ml (7 fl oz/¾ cup) milk or soya milk
50 g (2 oz/¼ cup) vegetable margarine
50 ml (2 fl oz/¼ cup) sunflower oil
150 g (5 oz/¾ cup) caster sugar
300 g (10 oz/2½ cups) plain flour
5 teaspoons baking powder
50 g (2 oz/½ cup) carob powder

❀ Creaming method
❀ Cake tins: two 20 cm (8") round tins, greased and floured
❀ Oven temperature: 180°C (350°F/Gas Mark 4)
❀ Baking time: 20–25 minutes

Mix the lemon juice and the milk and leave it to curdle. Beat the margarine, the oil and the sugar until the mixture is fluffy and creamy. Add the flour, baking powder, carob powder and mix. Stir in the sour milk gradually and continue beating for another two minutes.

Spoon the mixture into the prepared tins and bake for 20 minutes. Check if the centre of the cake is dry. If it is not, leave in the oven for another 5 minutes. Remove from the oven and allow to cool for 10 minutes. Turn out onto a wire cooling rack. Let it cool completely before filling.

Filling and icing ideas: Fudge Icing, Mixed Nuts Filling, Ricotta Icing, Ganache, Soft Cheese Icing.

Mock Chocolate Cake

Vegan

50 g (2 oz/½ cup) carob powder
50 ml (2 fl oz/¼ cup) hot water
1 tablespoon lemon juice
150 ml (5 fl oz/⅔ cup) milk or soya milk
100 g (3½ oz/½ cup) vegetable margarine
150 g (5 oz/¾ cup) caster sugar
200 g (7 oz/1½ cups) plain flour
½ teaspoon bicarbonate of soda
1 teaspoon baking powder
1 teaspoon vanilla essence

❀ Creaming method
❀ Cake tins: two 20 cm (8") round tins, greased and floured
❀ Oven temperature: 180°C (350°F/Gas Mark 4)
❀ Baking time: 20 minutes

In a cup or small bowl, dissolve the carob powder in the hot water. Leave it to cool for a few minutes. In another cup or bowl, mix the lemon juice and milk. Leave for a few minutes until the milk is sour. Cream the margarine and sugar until light and fluffy. Sift together the flour, bicarbonate of soda and baking powder. Add it to the creamed margarine and sugar, alternating with the soured milk. Add the dissolved carob and the vanilla essence and mix thoroughly.

Spoon the mixture into the tins. Bake for 20 minutes in the centre of the oven. Check if the cake is dry and cooked. If not, leave for a few more minutes. Allow the cake to cool in the tins for 10 minutes. Turn out and allow to cool completely before filling or icing with Chantilly Cream, Ricotta Icing, Ganache, Soft Cheese Icing or Tofu Icing.

Caramel Cake

VEGAN

100 g (3½ oz/¾ cup) soft brown sugar
100 ml (3½ fl oz/½ cup) hot water
50 ml (2 fl oz/¼ cup) sunflower oil
50 ml (2 fl oz/¼ cup) yoghurt or soya yoghurt
200 g (7 oz/1½ cups) self-raising flour
1 teaspoon baking powder

❀ Melting method
❀ Cake tins: two 20 cm (8") round tins, greased and floured
❀ Oven temperature: 180°C (350°F/Gas Mark 4)
❀ Baking time: 20–25 minutes

In a heavy saucepan, heat the sugar until it melts. Stir constantly with a spoon until the sugar changes colour. Add the hot water and mix. Allow to cool. Add the sunflower oil and the yoghurt.

Sift the flour and baking powder into a bowl. Pour the liquid mixture on top and beat with a spoon for 1 minute.

Bake for 20 minutes. Check if the centre of the cake is dry. If it is not, leave in the oven for another 5 minutes. Remove from the oven and allow to cool for 10 minutes. Turn out onto a wire cooling rack. Let it cool completely before filling with Fudge Icing.

Coffee and Walnut Cake

VEGAN

1 tablespoon instant barley coffee
2 tablespoons boiling water
200 ml (7 fl oz/¾ cup) milk or soya milk
50 ml (2 fl oz/¼ cup) sunflower oil
200 g (7 oz/1½ cups) self-raising flour
2 teaspoons baking powder
100 g (3½ oz/½ cup) caster sugar
50 g (2 oz/¼ cup) chopped walnuts
50 g (2 oz/¼ cup) walnut halves for decoration

❁ Wet and dry method
❁ Cake tins: two 20 cm (8") round tins, greased and floured
❁ Oven temperature: 180°C (350°F/Gas Mark 4)
❁ Baking time: 20 minutes

Dissolve the barley coffee in the boiling water. Mix the coffee, milk and oil together. Sift the flour, baking powder and sugar into a mixing bowl. Stir in the walnuts. Combine the wet and dry mixtures and beat for one minute.

Spoon the mixture into the prepared tins and bake for 20 minutes. Check if the centre of the cake is dry. If it is not, leave in the oven for another 5 minutes. Remove from the oven and allow to cool for 10 minutes. Turn out onto a wire cooling rack. When cold, fill and ice with coffee-flavoured Butter Icing and decorate with walnut halves.

Mocha Cake

VEGAN

2 tablespoons instant barley coffee
250 ml (8 fl oz/1 cup) water
2 tablespoons carob powder
100 g (3½ oz/½ cup) caster sugar
200 g (7 oz/1½ cups) self-raising flour
2 teaspoons baking powder
90 ml (3 fl oz/6 tablespoons) sunflower oil

❀ One-step method
❀ Cake tins: two 20 cm (8") round tins, greased and floured
❀ Oven temperature: 190°C (375°F/Gas Mark 5)
❀ Baking time: 25 minutes

Prepare the coffee according to the instructions on the packet or jar. Dissolve the carob powder in the hot coffee. Leave it to cool.

In a mixing bowl, mix the sugar, the flour and the baking powder. Add the oil and the cold coffee. Beat for 1 minute with a spoon. Spoon into the prepared cake tins. Bake for 25 minutes. Check if the centre of the cake is dry. If it is not, leave in the oven for another 5 minutes.

Remove from the oven and allow to cool for 10 minutes. Turn out onto a wire cooling rack. Let it cool completely before filling.

Filling ideas: Chantilly Cream, Vegan Cream, Butter Icing (coffee or chocolate flavour), Soft Cheese Icing.

Royal Orange Cake

VEGAN

150 g (5 oz/1¼ cups) plain flour, sifted
½ teaspoon bicarbonate of soda
1 teaspoon baking powder
100 ml (3½ fl oz/½ cup) sunflower oil
100 g (3½ oz/½ cup) caster sugar
50 ml (2 fl oz/¼ cup) yoghurt or soya yoghurt
100 ml (3½ fl oz/½ cup) orange juice

❁ Creaming method
❁ Cake tins: two 20 cm (8") round tins, greased and floured
❁ Oven temperature: 180°C (350°F/Gas Mark 4)
❁ Baking time: 25–30 minutes

Sift the flour, bicarbonate of soda and baking powder. In another mixing bowl, cream together the oil, sugar and yoghurt. Add the juice and the flour, and mix. Pour the mixture into the prepared cake tins.

Bake the cake for 25–30 minutes. Check if the centre of the cake is dry. If it is not, leave in the oven for another 5 minutes. Remove from the oven and allow to cool for 10 minutes. Turn out onto a wire cooling rack. When cold, sandwich the two cakes together with Orange Icing or See-through Icing.

Shepherd's Cake

one 400 g tin (14 oz tin/approx. 1½ cups) condensed milk
400 ml (14 fl oz/1½ cups) milk
200 ml (7 fl oz/¾ cup) honey
1 teaspoon ground cinnamon
1 teaspoon ground cloves
300 g (10 oz/2½ cups) plain flour or equal quantities of wholemeal and plain flour
2 teaspoons baking powder
1 teaspoon bicarbonate of soda

❈ One-step method
❈ Cake tins: two 25 cm (10") round sandwich tins, or one deep
    25 cm (10") tin, greased and floured
❈ Oven temperature: 180°C (350°F/Gas Mark 4)
❈ Baking time: 25–30 minutes

Mix the condensed milk, milk, honey, cinnamon and cloves. Sift the flour, baking powder and bicarbonate of soda on top and beat for one minute with a spoon. Pour the mixture into the prepared tins.

Bake for 25 minutes. Check if the centre of the cake is dry. If it is not, leave in the oven for another 5 minutes. Remove from the oven and allow to cool for 10 minutes. Turn out onto a wire cooling rack. Let it cool completely before filling.

Filling ideas: jam, Mixed Nut Filling, Fruit and Nut Filling, Peanut Butter Filling.

Quick Yoghurt Sponge

VEGAN

200 g (7 oz/1½ cups) self-raising flour
2 teaspoons baking powder
100 g (3½ oz/½ cup) caster sugar
150 ml (5 fl oz/⅔ cup) yoghurt or soya yoghurt
5 tablespoons sunflower oil
1 teaspoon vanilla essence

❀ Dry and wet method
❀ Cake tins: two 18 cm (7") round sandwich tins, greased and floured
❀ Oven temperature: 180°C (350°F/ Gas Mark 4)
❀ Baking time: 20 minutes

Sift flour, baking powder and sugar together. In a separate bowl, combine the yoghurt, oil and vanilla essence.

Combine the two mixtures and beat for a minute with a spoon. Pour into prepared tins. Bake for 20 minutes. Remove from the oven and allow to cool for 10 minutes. Turn out onto a wire cooling rack. Let it cool completely before filling.

Filling ideas: Fruit and Nut Filling, jam.

Velvet Cake

Vegan

200 g (7 oz/1½ cups) plain flour
200 g (7 oz/1 cup) caster sugar
2 teaspoons baking powder
1 teaspoon bicarbonate of soda
75 g (2½ oz/¾ cup) carob powder
200 ml (7 fl oz/¾ cup) warm water
2 tablespoons lemon juice
100 ml (3½ fl oz/½ cup) sunflower oil
½ teaspoon vanilla essence

❋ Dry and wet method
❋ Cake tins: two 20 cm (8") round tins, greased and floured
❋ Oven temperature: 180°C (350°F/Gas Mark 4)
❋ Baking time: 25 minutes

In a mixing bowl, sift the flour, sugar, baking powder, bicarbonate of soda and carob powder. In another mixing bowl, mix the water, lemon juice, oil and vanilla. Combine the two mixtures and beat with a spoon for two minutes.

Bake for 25 minutes. Check if the centre of the cake is dry. If it is not, leave in the oven for another 5 minutes. Remove from the oven and allow to cool for 10 minutes. Turn out onto a wire cooling rack. Let it cool completely before filling.

Filling and icing ideas: Chantilly Cream or Vegan Cream, Fudge Icing.

Genoese Cake

VEGAN

75 g (2½ oz/⅓ cup) butter or vegetable margarine
1 tablespoon lemon juice
2 tablespoons cold water
½ teaspoon vanilla essence
1 tablespoon cornflour
150 g (5 oz/1¼ cups) self-raising flour
1½ teaspoon baking powder
150 g (5 oz/¾ cup) caster sugar
1 tablespoon caster or icing sugar (for dredging)

❋ Melting method
❋ Cake tins: one 18 cm (7") round tin, greased and floured
❋ Oven temperature: 190°C (375°F/Gas Mark 5)
❋ Baking time: 20 minutes

Melt the butter or margarine over low heat. Pour into a mixing bowl and allow to cool. Stir in the lemon juice, water, vanilla and cornflour. Sift the dry ingredients together and fold them gently into the wet mixture.

Spoon the mixture into the prepared tin and place it at the centre of a preheated oven for 20 minutes. Check if the centre of the cake is dry. If it is not, leave for another 5 minutes. Remove from the oven and allow to cool for 10 minutes. Turn out onto a wire cooling rack.

Dredge with icing or caster sugar. Serve plain or, when cold, cut in two layers and fill with whipped cream and jam.

Ginger Sandwich Cake

125 g (4 oz/½ cup) soft butter or vegetable margarine
50 g (2 oz/¼ cup) sugar
2 tablespoons honey, diluted in 2 tablespoons hot water
50 ml (2 fl oz/¼ cup) condensed milk
200 g (7 oz/1½ cups) plain flour
2 teaspoons baking powder
1 tablespoon fresh ground ginger
½ teaspoon ground cinnamon
1 teaspoon bicarbonate of soda, dissolved in 2 tablespoons milk

❀ Creaming method
❀ Cake tins: two 20 cm (8") round tins, greased and floured
❀ Oven temperature: 180°C (350°F/Gas Mark 4)
❀ Baking time: 25–30 minutes

Cream the margarine and the sugar. Add the honey dissolved in the water and mix well. Add the condensed milk and beat until the mixture is creamy and light. Sift the flour, baking powder and spices on top and mix well. Finally, add the dissolved bicarbonate of soda.

Spoon the mixture into the prepared cake tins and bake for 25 minutes. Check if the centre of the cake is dry. If it is not, leave in the oven for another 5 minutes.

Remove from the oven and allow to cool for 10 minutes. Turn out onto a wire cooling rack. When cold, sandwich the two cakes together with Chantilly Cream or Soft Cheese Icing.

Vegan Sponge

VEGAN

200 g (7 oz/1½ cups) wholemeal flour, sifted
3 teaspoons baking powder
½ teaspoon salt
100 g (3½ oz/½ cup) muscovado sugar
200 ml (7 fl oz/¾ cup) soya milk
4 tablespoons sunflower seed oil
½ teaspoon vanilla essence

❀ Dry and wet method
❀ Cake tins: two 20 cm (8") round tins, greased and floured
❀ Oven temperature: 180°C (350°F/Gas Mark 4)
❀ Baking time: 20–25 minutes

Sift the flour, the baking powder and the salt in a mixing bowl. In another mixing bowl, dissolve the muscovado sugar in the soya milk. Add the oil and the vanilla. Mix well.

Combine the two mixtures and beat for one minute. Spoon the batter into the prepared tins. Bake for 20 minutes. Check if the cakes are dry in the centre. If they are not, leave in the oven for another 5 minutes.

Let the cakes cool for 10 minutes before turning out. When the cakes are cold, sandwich them together with Vegan Cream or Aduki Bean Filling.

Sugarfree Sponge Cake

VEGAN

This cake is not as soft as other sponges. However, this is an excellent recipe for people
who need to follow special diets.

150 g (5 oz/1 cup) raisins or chopped dates
150 ml (5 fl oz/⅔ cup) fruit juice
200 g (7 oz/1½ cups) self-raising flour
2 teaspoons baking powder
4 tablespoons sunflower oil
50 ml (2 fl oz/¼ cup) yoghurt or soya yoghurt

❈ One-step method
❈ Cake tins: two 20 cm (8") round tins, greased and floured
❈ Oven temperature: 180°C (350°F/Gas Mark 4)
❈ Baking time: 30–35 minutes

Soak the raisins or dates in the fruit juice and leave for a few hours if possible. Put
the fruit and juice in a blender and liquidize until the fruit forms a paste. Add the
remaining ingredients and blend for another minute. If you do not have a blender, boil
the fruit in water for approximately 20 minutes, mash it with a potato masher, let it cool
and then add the juice and the other ingredients.

Pour the mixture into the prepared cake tins and bake for 30 minutes. Check if the
centre of the cake is dry. If it is not, leave in the oven for another 5 minutes.

Remove from the oven and allow to cool for 10 minutes. Turn out onto a wire
cooling rack. When cold, join the two cakes together with Fruit and Nut Filling, Fruit
Filling or Tofu Icing.

Ekadashi Fruit Cake

Vegan

50 g (2 oz/½ cup) potato flour
200 g (7 oz/1½ cups) buckwheat flour or quinoa flour or a mixture of the two
1 teaspoon ground ginger
½ teaspoon each: cinnamon, ground cloves, nutmeg
1 teaspoon bicarbonate of soda
100 g (3½ oz/¾ cup) mixed dried fruit
the juice of 2 lemons and the rind of 1 lemon, finely grated
150 g (5 oz/¾ cup) muscovado sugar
200 ml (7 fl oz/¾ cup) milk or apple juice
50 ml (2 fl oz/¼ cup) sunflower oil

✤ Dry and wet method
✤ Cake tins: two 20 cm (8") round tins or one 1 kg (2 lb) loaf tin, greased
✤ Oven temperature: 180°C (350°F/Gas Mark 4)
✤ Baking time: 25–30 minutes

In a mixing bowl, sift the potato and buckwheat flours, the spices and the bicarbonate of soda. Mix in the fruit and the grated lemon rind. In a separate bowl, dissolve the sugar in the milk or apple juice. Add the oil and the lemon juice. Combine the two mixtures and beat for 1 minute.

Spoon the mixture into the prepared tins and bake for 25–30 minutes. Check if the centre is dry before removing from the oven. Leave to cool for 10 minutes before turning out. Join the two cakes together with one of the fillings below. If using a loaf tin, cut the cake in half horizontally and join the two halves with filling.

Filling and icing ideas: Ricotta Icing, Chantilly Cream, Soft Cheese Icing.

Lemon Sponge

VEGAN

200 g (7 oz/1½ cups) self-raising flour
2 teaspoons baking powder
100 g (3½ oz/½ cup) caster sugar
200 ml (7 fl oz/¾ cup) milk or soya milk
75 ml (2½ fl oz/5 tablespoons) sunflower oil
the juice and finely grated rind of 1 lemon

✤ Filling and icing:
500 ml (1 pint/2 cups) milk or soya milk
75 g (3 oz/½ cup) plain flour
75 g (3 oz/⅓ cup) sugar
1 teaspoon vanilla essence
the rind of 1 lemon, finely grated
2 tablespoons any sieved citrus fruit marmalade or jam

✤ Decoration:
2 tablespoons chopped mixed peel or slivers of lime or lemon rind

✤ Dry and wet method
✤ Cake tins: two 20 cm (8") round tins, greased and floured
✤ Oven temperature: 180°C (350°F/Gas Mark 4)
✤ Baking time: 20–25 minutes

In a mixing bowl, sift the flour, baking powder and sugar. In a measuring jug, measure and mix the milk, oil, juice and grated rind. Combine the two mixtures and beat with a spoon for 2 minutes. Spoon into the prepared tins and bake for 20 minutes. Check if the centre of the cake is dry. If it is not, leave in the oven for another 5 minutes.

Remove from the oven and allow to cool for 10 minutes. Turn out onto a wire cooling rack. Let it cool completely before filling and icing.

For the icing, pour the milk into a saucepan, but keep about ½ cup in a small bowl. Heat the milk in the saucepan and allow to boil. Add the flour and sugar to the milk in the bowl and stir until well blended. When the milk in the saucepan has boiled, add the flour mixture and stir vigorously until thick. Remove from the heat and stir in the essence and lemon rind.

Place one of the cakes on a serving plate and spread the sieved jam over the top. Spread with 4–5 tablespoons filling and allow to cool for 5 minutes. Place the other cake on top. Pour about half of the filling mixture slowly over the top, little by little, allowing it to drip over the sides. Allow to set for 2–3 minutes and pour the rest in the same way. Decorate with chopped peel or slivers of lime or lemon rind.

Honey Sponge

This recipe can be adapted for most sizes and shapes of baking tins. The recipe calls for a mixture of cornflour/cornstarch and water, which works as a binding ingredient.

On the following page are tables indicating the quantities for various size cakes and baking tins.

❀ Creaming method
❀ Cake tins: follow the table opposite (tins should be greased and floured)
❀ Oven temperature: 180°C (350°F/Gas Mark 4)

In a mixing bowl, beat the margarine, the sugar and the honey. Sift the flour and the baking powder on top. Mix well. In a cup, mix the cornflour with the water. Add this mixture to the bowl gradually, mixing constantly.

Pour the mixture into the prepared cake tin, and bake for the necessary time. Check if the centre of the cake is dry. If it is not, leave in the oven for another 5 minutes.

Remove from the oven and allow to cool for 10 minutes. Turn out onto a wire cooling rack. Let it cool completely before filling and icing it.

Filling ideas: Fruit and Nut Filling, Fruit Filling, Fudge Icing, jam.

Flour	Baking Powder	Sugar	Vegetable Margarine	Honey	Water + Cornflour
100 g (3½ oz/ ¾ cup)	1 tsp	50 g (2 oz/ ¼ cup)	30 g (1 oz/ 2 Tbsp)	1 Tbsp	100 ml (3½ fl oz/ + 1 Tbsp)
200 g (7 oz/ 1½ cups)	1½ tsp	100 g (3½ oz/ ½ cup)	75 g (2½ oz/ ⅓ cup)	1½ Tbsp	150 ml (5 fl oz/ + 1½ Tbsp)
300 g (10 oz/ 2½ cups)	2 tsp	150 g (5 oz/ ¾ cup)	100 g (3½ oz/ ½ cup)	2 Tbsp	250 ml (8 fl oz/ + 2 Tbsp)
400 g (14 oz/ 3 cups)	3 tsp	200 g (7 oz/ 1 cup)	150 g (5 oz/ ¾ cup)	3 Tbsp	300 ml (10 fl oz/ + 3 Tbsp)

Flour	Baking Tin	Baking Time
100 g (3½ oz/ ¾ cups)	one 18 cm/ 7" round tin or 12 cup cakes	15 minutes
200 g (7 oz/ 1½ cups)	one 25 cm/ 10" round tin or 24 cup cakes	15–20 minutes
300 g (10 oz/ 2½ cups)	two 20 cm/ 8" sponge tins or one 20 × 30 cm/ 8" × 12" rectangular tin	20 minutes
400 g (14 oz/ 3 cups)	one large 25 × 35 cm/ 10" × 14" rectangular tin	20–25 minutes

Quick Mix Sponge

VEGAN

This is the easiest and most versatile recipe you're likely to come across. It offers unlimited possibilities of variations and combinations. It is also easily adapted to different size cakes. Opposite is a table of proportions.

200 g (7 oz/1½ cups) self-raising flour
2 teaspoons baking powder
100 g (3½ oz/½ cup) caster sugar or soft brown sugar
200 ml (7 fl oz/¾ cup) yoghurt or soya yoghurt
5 tablespoons sunflower oil
1 teaspoon vanilla essence

❀ Dry and wet method
❀ Cake tins: Follow the table (tins should be greased and floured)
❀ Oven temperature: 180°C (350°F/Gas Mark 4)

Sift flour, baking powder and sugar into a large bowl. In a measuring jug, combine the yoghurt, oil and vanilla essence. Combine the two mixtures and beat for two minutes.

Spoon into prepared tins. Bake for time recommended in the table opposite. Leave to cool completely before icing.

❀ Variations:
Orange: substitute the vanilla essence for the juice and grated rind of one small orange. Carob: add 1½ tablespoons carob powder diluted in 1½ tablespoons hot water to the wet mixture. Coconut: add 1½ tablespoons dried shredded coconut to the dry mixture. Walnut: add 1½ tablespoons finely chopped walnuts to the dry mixture.

Flour	Baking	Sugar	Oil	Yoghurt	Carob	Essence
150 g	1½ tsp	75 g	3 Tbsp	150 ml	1 Tbsp	1/2 tsp
200 g	2 tsp	100 g	5 Tbsp	200 ml	1½ Tbsp	1 tsp
300 g	3 tsp	150 g	100 ml	300 ml	2 Tbsp	11/2 tsp

Flour	Baking Tin	Baking Time
150 g (5 oz/1¼ cups)	one 18 cm/ 7" round tin or 12 cup cakes	15–20 minutes
200 g (7 oz/1½ cups)	two 20 cm/ 8" sandwich tins or 24 cup cakes	15–20 minutes
300 g (10 oz/2½ cups)	two 25 cm/ 10" sponge tins or one 20 × 30 cm/ 8" × 12" rectangular tin	20 minutes

Ekadashi Sponge

Vegan

50 g (2 oz/½ cup) potato flour
200 g (7 oz/1½ cups) buckwheat flour or quinoa flour or a mixture of the two
1 teaspoon ground ginger
1½ teaspoons bicarbonate of soda
150 g (5 oz/¾ cup) caster sugar
200 ml (7 fl oz/¾ cup) milk or apple juice
the juice of 1 lemon
50 ml (2 fl oz/¼ cup) sunflower oil
the juice and the finely grated rind of 1 medium orange

❈ Dry and wet method
❈ Cake tins: two 20 cm (8") round tins, greased, or 24 fairy cake cups
❈ Oven temperature: 180°C (350°F/Gas Mark 4)
❈ Baking time: 15–20 minutes

In a mixing bowl, sift the potato and buckwheat flours, the ginger and the bicarbonate of soda. Mix in the sugar. In a different bowl, mix together the milk or apple juice and the lemon juice. Add the oil, orange rind and juice. Combine the two mixtures and beat for one minute.

Spoon the mixture into the prepared tins and bake for 15–20 minutes. Check if the cakes are dry in the centre before removing from the oven. Leave them to cool for 10 minutes before turning out. Leave them to cool completely before filling and icing.

Filling and icing ideas: Fudge Icing, Chantilly Cream, Soft Cheese Filling.

Cream Sponge

250 ml (8 fl oz/1 cup) whipping or double cream
200 g (7 oz/1½ cup) plain flour
2 teaspoons baking powder
100 g (3½ oz/½ cup) caster sugar
150 ml (5 fl oz/⅔ cup) yoghurt
2 teaspoons lemon juice
1 teaspoon vanilla essence

❀ Creaming method
❀ Cake tins: two 20 cm (8") round tins, greased and floured
❀ Oven temperature: 180°C (350°F/Gas Mark 4)
❀ Baking time: 30–35 minutes

In a mixing bowl, whip the cream. In another mixing bowl, sift the flour, baking powder and sugar. Gradually add the yoghurt, lemon juice and vanilla. Fold in the whipped cream.

Spoon the mixture into the prepared cake tins. Bake for 30 minutes. Check if the centre of the cake is dry. If it is not, leave in the oven for another 5 minutes.

Remove from the oven and allow to cool for 10 minutes. Turn out onto a wire cooling rack. Let it cool completely before filling.

Filling ideas: Chantilly Cream, jam, Butter Icing, Shrikhand Filling.

Party Sponge

VEGAN

300 g (10 oz/2½ cups) flour
3 teaspoons baking powder
½ teaspoon bicarbonate of soda
200 g (7 oz/1 cup) caster sugar
50 g (2 oz/½ cup) carob powder
2 tablespoons lemon juice
75 ml (2½ fl oz/⅓ cup) yoghurt or soya yoghurt
100 ml (3½ fl oz/½ cup) sunflower oil
200 ml (7 fl oz/¾ cup) water

❊ Dry and wet method
❊ Cake tins: two 20 cm (8") round tins, greased and floured
❊ Oven temperature: 180°C (350°F/Gas Mark 4)
❊ Baking time: 20 minutes

In a mixing bowl, sift the flour, baking powder, bicarbonate of soda, sugar and carob powder. In another mixing bowl, mix the lemon, the yoghurt, the oil and the water. Combine the two mixtures and beat with a spoon.

Bake for about 20 minutes. Check if the centre of the cake is dry. Remove from the oven and allow to cool for 10 minutes. Turn out onto a wire cooling rack. Let it cool completely before filling.

Filling and icing ideas: Chantilly Cream or Vegan Cream, Butter Icing, Crème Pâtisserie (vegan).

SQUARES, WEDGES AND SLICES

These cakes are usually baked in flat, rectangular cake tins, also known as slab cake tins. A roasting tin or a deep Swiss roll tin, of about 20 × 30 × 4 cm (8" × 12" × 1½"), may be used instead. The cakes may be iced in different ways, but they are rarely filled. Most of the recipes in the previous section can also be baked in this way. When cold, the cakes can be cut into squares, diamonds or rectangles. If using a round cake tin, cut the cake in wedges. These cakes are easy to transport and are therefore wonderful for picnics and lunch boxes.

Brownies

VEGAN

100 ml (3½ fl oz/½ cup) yoghurt or soya yoghurt
100 g (3½ oz/½ cup) caster or muscovado sugar
50 ml (2 fl oz/¼ cup) sunflower oil
100 g (3½ oz/¾ cup) self-raising flour
15 g (½ oz/2 tablespoons) carob powder
a pinch of salt
½ teaspoon baking powder
100 g (3½ oz/½ cup) carob drops or carob pieces or Mock Chocolate
100 g (3½ oz/½ cup) chopped walnuts (optional)

❀ Creaming method
❀ Cake tin: one Swiss roll tin, approx. 20 × 30 cm (8" × 12")
 or one 20 cm (8") square tin, greased and floured
❀ Oven temperature: 180°C (350°F/Gas Mark 4)
❀ Baking time: 20–25 minutes

In a mixing bowl, beat the yoghurt, the sugar and the oil. Sift the flour, carob powder, salt and baking powder on top and mix.

Place the carob drops or pieces in a bowl and melt them over a saucepan of hot water. Add this to the mixture and beat with a spoon. Stir in the walnuts.

Spoon the mixture into the prepared cake tin. Bake the cake for 20 minutes if using a Swiss roll tin; 25 minutes for a deeper, square tin. Remove from the oven and allow to cool for 10 minutes. Turn out onto a wire cooling rack. When cold, cut into squares.

For special occasions, spread Butter Icing (chocolate flavour) before cutting. Cut into squares and decorate each square with a walnut half.

Banana Cake

VEGAN

4 medium bananas, sliced
the juice of 1 lemon
300 g (10 oz/2½ cups) self-raising flour
2 teaspoons baking powder
150 g (5 oz/1 cup) soft brown sugar
1 teaspoon ground cinnamon
100 ml (3½ fl oz/½ cup) yoghurt or soya yoghurt
200 ml (7 fl oz/¾ cup) milk or soya milk
100 ml (3½ fl oz/½ cup) sunflower oil
2 medium bananas, chopped
1 tablespoon sugar, mixed with ½ teaspoon ground cinnamon

❀ One-step method
❀ Cake tin: one 20 × 30 cm (8" × 12") rectangular tin, greased and floured
❀ Oven temperature: 180°C (350°F/Gas Mark 4)
❀ Baking time: 25–30 minutes

In a small mixing bowl, toss the banana slices and the lemon juice. Set aside. In a bigger mixing bowl, sift the flour and the baking powder. Stir in the sugar, cinnamon and yoghurt. Gradually, add the milk and the oil and beat with a spoon. Mix in the chopped bananas.

Pour the mixture into the prepared cake tin. Arrange the banana slices on top and sprinkle with the sugar and cinnamon mixture. Bake the cake for 25 to 30 minutes. Allow it to cool in the tin for 30 minutes. Cut into squares or rectangles.

Banana and Cherry Cake

VEGAN

200 g (7 oz/1½ cups) self-raising flour
2 teaspoons baking powder
2 tablespoons honey or molasses
4 tablespoons sunflower oil
150 ml (5 fl oz/⅔ cup) fruit juice
100 g (3½ oz/½ cup) caster sugar
2 bananas, chopped
½ cup cherries (tinned or fresh), drained and chopped

❀ Dry and wet method
❀ Cake tin: one 20 × 30 cm (8" × 12") rectangular tin, greased and floured
❀ Oven temperature: 180°C (350°F/Gas Mark 4)
❀ Baking time: 25–30 minutes

In a large mixing bowl, sift the flour and the baking powder. In a smaller mixing bowl, mix the honey or molasses, the oil, juice and sugar. Combine the two mixtures and mix well. Stir in the chopped bananas and cherries.

Pour the mixture into the prepared cake tin. Bake the cake for 25 to 30 minutes. Let the cake cool in the tin for about 30 minutes. Cut into squares or rectangles.

Butterscotch Cake

VEGAN

150 g (5 oz/¾ cup) caster sugar
100 ml (3½ fl oz/½ cup) boiling water
a pinch of salt
3 tablespoons vegetable margarine
100 ml (3½ fl oz/½ cup) yoghurt or soya yoghurt
½ teaspoon vanilla essence
200 ml (7 fl oz/¾ cup) milk or soya milk
250 g (½ lb/2 cups) self-raising flour
2 teaspoons baking powder

❉ One-step method
❉ Cake tin: one 20 × 30 cm (8" × 12") rectangular tin, greased and floured
❉ Oven temperature: 180°C (350°F/Gas Mark 4)
❉ Baking time: 25–30 minutes

In a heavy-bottomed saucepan, place half the sugar over a low fire. When the sugar has melted and is golden in colour, add the boiling water and salt and mix well. Set aside and allow to cool slightly.

In a mixing bowl, beat together the margarine, yoghurt, vanilla, milk and the rest of the sugar. Add the sugar mixture and mix well. Mix in the flour and the baking powder. Spoon into the prepared cake tin and bake for 25 to 30 minutes.

Remove from the oven and allow to cool for 10 minutes. Turn out onto a wire cooling rack. When cold, ice the cake with Fudge Icing or Butter Icing and cut it into squares or rectangles.

Spicy Carrot Cake

VEGAN

100 g (3½ oz/¾ cup) plain flour
1 teaspoon baking powder
1 teaspoon bicarbonate of soda
100 g (3½ oz/½ cup) caster sugar
100 ml (3½ fl oz/½ cup) yoghurt or soya yoghurt
50 g (2 oz/¼ cup) butter or vegetable margarine, softened
150 g (5 oz/1 cup) grated carrots
50 g (2 oz/¼ cup) chopped Brazil nuts
50 g (2 oz/¼ cup) raisins (optional)
¼ teaspoon ground cardamom seeds (optional)
¼ teaspoon ground ginger or 1 teaspoon fresh grated ginger

❀ One-step method
❀ Cake tin: one 20 cm (8") square tin, greased and floured
❀ Oven temperature: 180°C (350°F/Gas Mark 4)
❀ Baking time: 30 minutes

Sift the flour, the baking powder and the bicarbonate of soda. Add the sugar, yoghurt and butter and mix. Add the carrot, chopped nuts, raisins and spices. Mix with a spoon and pour the mixture into the prepared cake tin.

Bake the cake for 30 minutes. Check if the centre of the cake is dry. If it is not, leave in the oven for another 5 minutes. Remove from the oven and allow to cool for 10 minutes. Turn out onto a wire cooling rack. When cold, if you wish, ice with Ricotta Icing or Tofu Icing and cut into squares or rectangles.

Coconut Cake

Vegan

3 tablespoons butter or vegan margarine
100 g (3½ oz/½ cup) caster sugar
200 g (7 oz/1½ cups) self-raising flour
2 teaspoons baking powder
200 ml (7 fl oz/¾ cup) coconut milk or milk mixed up with 3 tablespoons
    grated coconut
½ teaspoon vanilla essence
1 tablespoon lemon juice
1 tablespoon lemon rind

❀ Topping:
one 200 g tin (7 oz tin/approx. ¾ cup) condensed milk
100 g (3½ oz/1 cup) grated coconut

❀ Creaming method
❀ Cake tin: one 20 × 30 cm (8" × 12") rectangular tin, greased and floured
❀ Oven temperature: 180°C (350°F/Gas Mark 4)
❀ Baking time: 25–30 minutes

In a mixing bowl, cream the butter and the sugar. Gradually, add the flour, the baking powder and the coconut milk. Stir in the vanilla, lemon juice and rind.

Pour the mixture into the prepared cake tin. Bake the cake for 25 to 30 minutes. Let the cake cool in the cake tin for about half an hour. Prick the whole cake with a fork. Spread the condensed milk and let it be absorbed by the cake. Sprinkle with the grated coconut. Cut into squares or rectangles.

Polenta Cake

VEGAN

100 g (3½ oz/¾ cup) plain flour
100 g (3½ oz/½ cup) polenta flour
4 teaspoons baking powder
100 g (3½ oz/½ cup) caster sugar
50 ml (2 fl oz/¼ cup) yoghurt or soya yoghurt
3 tablespoons sunflower oil
200 ml (7 fl oz/¾ cup) water
2 teaspoons ground fennel seeds
100 g (3½ oz/½ cup) grated Cheshire or other white hard cheese
　　or any hard soya cheese

❀ One-step method
❀ Cake tin: one 20 × 30 cm (8" × 12") rectangular tin, greased and floured
❀ Oven temperature: 180°C (350°F/Gas Mark 4)
❀ Baking time: 30–35 minutes

Sift together the plain flour, polenta flour and baking powder. Stir in the sugar, yoghurt, oil, water and ground fennel seeds. Add the cheese and beat with a spoon.

Pour the mixture into the prepared cake tin. Bake it for 30 minutes. Check if the centre of the cake is dry. If it is not, leave in the oven for another 5 minutes.

Remove from the oven and allow to cool for 10 minutes. Turn out onto a wire cooling rack. Let the cake cool completely before cutting into squares or rectangles.

Gokula Cake

VEGAN

4 tablespoons heaped butter or vegetable margarine
2 tablespoons honey or molasses
100 g (3½ oz/½ cup) caster sugar
200 ml (7 fl oz/¾ cup) milk or soya milk
300 g (10 oz/2½ cups) self-raising flour
3 teaspoons baking powder
100 g (3½ oz/1 cup) grated coconut
25 g (1 oz/¼ cup) cornflour

❀ Melting method
❀ Cake tin: one 20 × 30 cm (8" × 12") rectangular tin, greased and floured
❀ Oven temperature: 180°C (350°F/Gas Mark 4)
❀ Baking time: 25–30 minutes

Melt the butter in a saucepan over low heat. Remove it from the heat and stir in the honey and sugar. Mix in the milk and leave it to cool. In the meantime, sift the flour and baking powder into a large mixing bowl. Add half the amount of grated coconut.

When the wet mixture is cool, whisk in the cornflour. Combine the dry and wet mixtures and beat with a spoon.

Pour into the prepared cake tin. Sprinkle with the rest of the grated coconut. Bake for 25 minutes. Check if the centre of the cake is dry. If it is not, leave in the oven for another 5 minutes. Remove from the oven and allow to cool for 10 minutes. Turn out onto a wire cooling rack. When completely cool, cut into squares or rectangles.

Krishna Cake

VEGAN

100 g (3½ oz/½ cup) butter or vegetable margarine
2 tablespoons honey or golden syrup
100 g (3½ oz/¾ cup) raisins
100 g (3½ oz/½ cup) muscovado sugar
200 ml (7 fl oz/¾ cup) milk or whey or soya milk
300 g (10 oz/2½ cups) self-raising flour
3 teaspoons baking powder
50 g (2 oz/¼ cup) chopped mixed nuts
50 g (2 oz/½ cup) grated coconut
25 g (1 oz/2 tablespoons) cornflour, dissolved in 2 tablespoons cold water

❀ Melting method
❀ Cake tin: one 20 × 30 cm (8" × 12") rectangular tin, greased and floured
❀ Oven temperature: 180°C (350°F/Gas Mark 4)
❀ Baking time: 30–35 minutes

In a saucepan, melt the butter and stir in the honey. Remove from the heat and add the raisins, sugar and milk. Leave it to cool.

In a mixing bowl, sift the flour and baking powder. Add the nuts and the grated coconut. Add the wet mixture to the dry one. Mix in the cornflour diluted in water. Beat with a spoon for 1 minute.

Spoon the mixture into the prepared cake tin and bake for 30 minutes. Check if the centre of the cake is dry. If it is not, leave in the oven for another 5 minutes. Remove from the oven and allow to cool for 10 minutes. Turn out onto a wire cooling rack. When cold, cut into squares or rectangles.

Apple Cake

VEGAN

3 apples, sliced
the juice of 1 lemon
200 g (7 oz/1½ cups) self-raising flour
2 teaspoons baking powder
1 teaspoon ground cinnamon
100 g (3½ oz/¾ cup) soft brown sugar
200 ml (7 fl oz/¾ cup) milk or soya milk
75 ml (2½ fl oz/⅓ cup) sunflower oil
2 apples, chopped
1 tablespoon sugar, mixed with ½ teaspoon ground cinnamon

❀ One-step method
❀ Cake tin: one 20 × 30 cm (8" × 12") rectangular tin, greased and floured
❀ Oven temperature: 180°C (350°F/Gas Mark 4)
❀ Baking time: 25–30 minutes

In a small mixing bowl, toss the sliced apples with the lemon juice. In a larger mixing bowl, sift the flour, the baking powder and the cinnamon. Gradually add the sugar, milk and oil, and beat with a spoon. Stir in the chopped apples.

Pour or spoon the mixture into the prepared cake tin. Place the apple slices on top and sprinkle with the sugar and cinnamon mixture. Bake the cake for 25 to 30 minutes. Let it cool in the cake tin for 20 to 25 minutes. Cut into squares.

Ginger Squares

VEGAN

4 tablespoons vegetable margarine
100 ml (3½ fl oz/½ cup) molasses
100 g (3½ oz/½ cup) caster sugar
150 ml (5 fl oz/⅔ cup) milk or soya milk
50 ml (2 fl oz/¼ cup) yoghurt or soya yoghurt
200 g (7 oz/1½ cups) self-raising flour
2 teaspoons baking powder
1 teaspoon ground cinnamon
2 teaspoons ground ginger

❀ Melting method
❀ Cake tin: one 20 × 30 cm (8" × 12") rectangular tin, greased and floured
❀ Oven temperature: 180°C (350°F/Gas Mark 4)
❀ Baking time: 30–35 minutes

In a saucepan, melt the margarine and mix in the molasses. Remove from the heat and cool for a few minutes. Add the sugar, milk and yoghurt.

In a mixing bowl, sift the flour, baking powder, cinnamon and ginger. Pour the liquid mixture over the flour and beat for one minute with a spoon. Turn into the prepared cake tin and bake for 30 minutes. Check if the centre of the cake is dry. If it is not, leave the cake in the oven for another 5 minutes.

Remove from the oven and allow to cool for 10 minutes. Turn out onto a wire cooling rack. When cold, cut into squares.

Macrobiotic Cake

VEGAN

150 g (5 oz/1¼ cups) wholemeal flour
150 g (5 oz/1 cup) rice flour
4 teaspoons baking powder
½ teaspoon salt
50 g (2 oz/¼ cup) sesame seeds
50 g (2 oz/¼ cup) chopped almonds or Brazil nuts
100 g (3½ oz/¾ cup) raisins
2 medium apples, chopped
50 ml (2 fl oz/¼ cup) sunflower oil
250 ml (8 fl oz/1 cup) water

❀ One-step method
❀ Cake tin: one 20 × 30 cm (8" × 12") rectangular tin, greased and floured
❀ Oven temperature: 180°C (350°F/Gas Mark 4)
❀ Baking time: 35–40 minutes

Sift together the flours, baking powder and salt. Add the sesame seeds, chopped nuts and raisins, and mix thoroughly. Mix in the chopped apple, oil and water. Beat for a minute or two.

Spoon into the prepared cake tin. Bake the cake for 35 minutes. Check if the centre of the cake is dry. If it is not, leave the cake in the oven for another 5 minutes.

Remove from the oven and allow to cool for 10 minutes. Turn out onto a wire cooling rack. When cold, cut into squares.

As an alternative, ice with Aduki Bean Filling. Allow the icing to set and then cut the cake into squares.

Sweetcorn Cake

V EGAN

200 ml (7 fl oz/¾ cup) fennel seed tea
200 g (7 oz/1½ cups) plain flour
4 teaspoons baking powder
100 g (3½ oz/½ cup) caster sugar
100 g (3½ oz/½ cup) sweetcorn (fresh, frozen or tinned)
75 ml (2½ fl oz/⅓ cup) sunflower oil

❀ One-step method
❀ Cake tin: one 20 × 30 cm (8" × 12") rectangular tin, greased and floured
❀ Oven temperature: 180°C (350°F/Gas Mark 4)
❀ Baking time: 20–25 minutes

Make the fennel seed tea and allow it to cool. If using fresh sweetcorn, boil it for 10 minutes and allow it to cool. If using frozen, defrost it before mixing it into the cake.

Sift the flour and the baking powder. Add the sugar and the sweet corn and mix. Add the oil and the cold tea. Beat for one minute with a spoon.

Pour the mixture into the prepared cake tin. Bake for 20 minutes. Check if the centre of the cake is dry. If it is not, leave in the oven for another 5 minutes.

Remove from the oven and allow to cool for 10 minutes. Turn out onto a wire cooling rack. When cold, ice with Ricotta Icing or Sweetcorn Icing and cut into squares.

Oriental Cake

VEGAN

100 g (3½ oz/¾ cup) plain flour
100 g (3½ oz/¾ cup) wholemeal flour
½ teaspoon each ground cinnamon, ginger, cloves, nutmeg, star anise (or aniseed)
3 teaspoons baking powder
2 tablespoons vegetable margarine
2 tablespoons honey, agave syrup or golden syrup
2 tablespoons sunflower oil
2 tablespoons muscovado sugar
200 ml (7 fl oz/¾ cup) fruit juice (orange, apple, etc.)

❋ Creaming method
❋ Cake tin: one 18 × 25 cm (7" × 10") rectangular or one 20 cm (8") round tin, greased
  and floured
❋ Oven temperature: 180°C (350°F/Gas Mark 4)
❋ Baking time: 25–30 minutes

Sift together the flours, spices and baking powder. In a different mixing bowl, beat the margarine, honey, oil and sugar until light and fluffy. Gradually add the fruit juice, alternating each addition with spoonfuls of the sifted dry ingredients. Mix well with a spoon.

Turn the mixture into the prepared cake tin and bake for 25 minutes. Check if the centre of the cake is dry. If it is not, leave the cake in the oven for a few minutes longer.

Remove from the oven and allow to cool for 10 minutes. Turn out onto a wire cooling rack. When cold, cut into squares or wedges.

Lancashire Parkin

VEGAN

100 ml (3½ fl oz/½ cup) molasses or treacle
100 g (3½ oz/½ cup) vegetable margarine
100 g (3½ oz/½ cup) muscovado sugar
100 g (3½ oz/¾ cup) plain flour
100 g (3½ oz/¾ cup) wholemeal flour
1 teaspoon bicarbonate of soda
1 teaspoon ground ginger
100 g (3½ oz/1 cup) porridge (rolled) oats

❀ Melting method
❀ Cake tin: one 20 × 30 cm (8" × 12") rectangular tin, greased and lined with greaseproof paper
❀ Oven temperature: 180°C (350°F/Gas Mark 4)
❀ Baking time: 50–60 minutes

Place the molasses or treacle, the margarine and the sugar in a saucepan over low heat, stirring all the time with a spoon. When the margarine is melted and the ingredients blended, remove the saucepan from the heat and let the mixture cool slightly.

In a mixing bowl, sift the flours, bicarbonate of soda and ginger. Mix in the porridge oats. Pour the warm molasses mixture over the dry mixture and mix well.

Spoon the mixture into the prepared tin and bake for approximately 50 minutes. Check if the centre of the cake is dry. If it is not, leave the cake in the oven for a few minutes longer. Remove it from the oven and allow to cool for 10 minutes. Turn out onto a wire cooling rack. When cold, cut into squares.

Rhubarb Cake

VEGAN

100 g (3½ oz/½ cup) butter or vegetable margarine
150 g (5 oz/¾ cup) caster sugar
4 teaspoons vanilla sugar or 1 teaspoon vanilla essence
200 g (7 oz/1½ cups) plain flour
4 teaspoons baking powder
200 ml (7 fl oz/¾ cup) milk or soya milk
2 cups rhubarb, cut into 1.5 cm (½") pieces

✲ Topping:
50 g (2 oz/¼ cup) flour
50 g (2 oz/¼ cup) caster sugar
25 g (1 oz/2 tablespoons) butter or vegetable margarine
50 g (2 oz/¼ cup) chopped almonds

✲ Creaming method
✲ Cake tin: one 25 cm (10") round spring-clip tin, greased and floured
✲ Oven temperature: 180°C (350°F/Gas Mark 4)
✲ Baking time: 45 minutes

Cream the butter and sugar together until smooth. Add vanilla essence if using. In another bowl, sift together the flour, baking powder and vanilla sugar, if using. Mix in the milk and the butter mixture gradually. Turn into the prepared tin and cover with the rhubarb pieces. For the topping, mix the flour, sugar and butter together and crumble on top of the rhubarb. Sprinkle with chopped almonds.

Bake for 45 minutes, remove from the oven and allow to cool for 20 minutes before removing from the tin. Serve it plain or, on special occasions, with whipped cream.

Giant Jam Scone

VEGAN

A cross between a cake and a scone, this is delicious served with a cup of herbal tea on a cold afternoon.

200 g (7 oz/1½ cups) plain flour
3 teaspoons baking powder
50 g (2 oz/¼ cup) caster sugar
25 g (1 oz/2 tablespoons) butter or vegetable margarine
200 ml (7 fl oz/¾ cup) cold milk or soya milk
4 heaped tablespoons raspberry or your favourite jam

❂ Rub-in method
❂ Cake tin: one 20 cm (8") square tin, greased and floured
❂ Oven temperature: 180°C (350°F/Gas Mark 4)
❂ Baking time: 20–25 minutes

Sift together the flour, baking powder and sugar. Rub in the butter until the mixture resembles fine breadcrumbs. Make a well in the centre and add the milk, a little at a time, stirring constantly. Mix thoroughly until well blended.

Spoon half of the mixture into the prepared cake tin. Carefully spread the jam on top. Spoon the rest of the cake mixture over the jam, making sure to cover completely.

Bake the cake for approximately 20 minutes. Check if the centre of the cake is dry. If it is not, leave the cake in the oven for a few minutes longer. Remove it from the oven and allow to cool for 10 minutes. Turn out onto a wire cooling rack. Cut into squares and serve warm.

Raisin Cake

VEGAN

100 g (3½ oz/¾ cup) wholemeal flour
100 g (3½ oz/1 cup) cornflour
1 teaspoon cinnamon
2 teaspoons baking powder
200 ml (7 fl oz/¾ cup) yoghurt or soya yoghurt
1 tablespoon lemon juice
100 g (3½ oz/½ cup) caster or muscovado sugar
100 g (3½ oz/½ cup) soft butter or vegetable margarine
100 g (3½ oz/¾ cup) raisins

✿ Creaming method
✿ Cake tin: one 20 cm (8") square tin, greased and floured
✿ Oven temperature: 180°C (350°F/Gas Mark 4)
✿ Baking time: 30–35 minutes

In a mixing bowl, sift the flour, cornflour, cinnamon and baking powder. In a cup, combine the yoghurt and the lemon juice.

In another bowl, break up the sugar, if using muscovado. Beat the butter and the sugar until light and fluffy. Tip the yoghurt mixture into the creamed mixture, one spoonful at a time, adding one spoonful of the dry mixture with each spoon of yoghurt. Gently fold in the raisins.

Spread the mixture into the prepared cake tin. Bake the cake for 30 minutes. Check if the centre of the cake is dry. If it is not, leave in the oven for another 5 minutes.

Remove from the oven and allow to cool. Cut into squares.

Tofu Cake

Vegan

100 g (3½ oz/½ cup) tofu
100 ml (3½ fl oz/½ cup) sunflower oil
100 ml (3½ fl oz/½ cup) orange juice
1 teaspoon vanilla essence
100 ml (3½ fl oz/½ cup) molasses
150 g (5 oz/1¼ cups) wholemeal flour
100 g (3½ oz/¾ cup) plain flour
3 teaspoons baking powder
2 medium apples, peeled and sliced

❀ Dry and wet method
❀ Cake tin: one 20 × 30 cm (8" × 12") rectangular tin, greased and floured
❀ Oven temperature: 180°C (350°F/Gas Mark 4)
❀ Baking time: 45–50 minutes

With a fork, mash the tofu. Add the oil, juice, vanilla essence and molasses. In a mixing bowl, sift the flours and the baking powder. Combine the dry and wet mixtures and beat with a spoon.

Turn into the prepared cake tin and spread the sliced apples on top. Bake for 45 minutes. Check if the centre of the cake is dry. If it is not, leave the cake in the oven for a few minutes longer.

Remove from the oven and allow to cool for 10 minutes. Turn out onto a wire cooling rack. When cold, cut into squares.

Honey Squares

250 g (8 oz/2 cups) plain flour
3 teaspoons baking powder
2 teaspoons ground cloves
2 teaspoons ground cinnamon
100 g (3½ oz/½ cup) sugar
2 teaspoons grated lemon rind
2 teaspoons ground ginger
100 ml (3½ fl oz/½ cup) honey
60 ml (2 fl oz/¼ cup) sunflower oil
100 ml (3½ fl oz/½ cup) milk
100 ml (3½ fl oz/½ cup) cold camomile or fennel tea

❀ One-step method
❀ Cake tin: one 20 × 30 cm (8" × 12") rectangular tin, greased and floured
❀ Oven temperature: 180°C (350°F/Gas Mark 4)
❀ Baking time: 35 minutes

In a large mixing bowl, sift the flour, baking powder, cloves and cinnamon. Add the sugar, lemon rind and ginger. Gradually add the honey, oil, milk and tea. Mix thoroughly.

Pour or spoon the mixture into the prepared cake tin and bake for 35 minutes. Remove from the oven and allow to cool for 10 minutes. Turn out onto a wire cooling rack. When cold, cut into squares.

Apricot Cake

VEGAN

100 g (3½ oz/¾ cup) dried apricots
100 g (3½ oz/¾ cup) plain flour
2 teaspoon baking powder
50 g (2 oz/¼ cup) caster sugar
25 g (1 oz/2 tablespoons) butter or vegetable margarine
30 ml (1 fl oz/2 tablespoons) milk or soya milk
75 ml (2½ fl oz/⅓ cup) yoghurt or soya yoghurt

❋ Topping:
50 g (2 oz/⅓ cup) flour
15 g (½ oz/1 tablespoon) butter or vegetable margarine
50 g (2 oz/¼ cup) caster sugar
1 teaspoon ground cinnamon

❋ One-step method
❋ Cake tin: one 20 cm (8") square tin, greased and floured
❋ Oven temperature: 180°C (350°F/Gas Mark 4)
❋ Baking time: 30 minutes

Wash the apricots and soak them for at least four hours or overnight. In a mixing bowl, sift the flour and baking powder. Add the sugar, butter, milk and yoghurt. Beat with a spoon until well blended.

Turn into the prepared cake tin. Drain the apricots and chop them. Sprinkle them over the cake mixture.

For the topping, mix the flour and the butter using your fingertips until the mixture resembles fine breadcrumbs. Mix in the sugar and the cinnamon. Sprinkle this mixture over the apricots. Bake the cake for 30 minutes. Remove from the oven and allow to cool for half an hour. Cut into squares.

Orange and Carob Squares

300 g (10 oz/2½ cups) plain flour
6 teaspoons baking powder
100 g (3½ oz/1 cup) carob powder
100 g (3½ oz/¾ cup) raisins (optional)
100 ml (3½ oz/½ cup) honey
100 ml (3½ fl oz/½ cup) sunflower oil
200 ml (7 fl oz/¾ cup) orange juice
200 ml (7 fl oz/¾ cup) yoghurt
2 tablespoons grated orange rind

❀ Topping:
50 g (2 oz/¼ cup) caster sugar
15 g (½ oz/1 tablespoon) butter
50 g (2 oz/⅓ cup) flour
1 teaspoon ground cinnamon

❀ Dry and wet method
❀ Cake tin: one 20 × 30 cm (8" × 12") tin, greased and floured
❀ Oven temperature: 180°C (350°F/Gas Mark 4)
❀ Baking time: 25 minutes

In a mixing bowl, sift the flour, baking powder and carob powder. Mix in the raisins. In a second bowl, mix the honey and the oil. Mix in the orange juice gradually. Add the yoghurt and orange rind. Combine and beat with a spoon. Turn into the cake tin.

Mix the topping ingredients until the mixture resembles fine breadcrumbs. Sprinkle it over the cake.

Bake for 25 minutes. Let the cake cool in the tin for 20 minutes and cut into squares.

Gingerbread

VEGAN

This sticky, healthier version of traditional gingerbread can be cut into shapes in order to make a gingerbread house.

50 g (2 oz/¼ cup) butter or vegetable margarine
200 ml (7 fl oz/¾ cup) molasses
100 ml (3½ fl oz/⅔ cup) milk or soya milk
200 g (7 oz/1½ cups) plain flour
a pinch of salt
1½ teaspoons baking powder
½ teaspoon bicarbonate of soda
2 teaspoons ground ginger
50 g (2 oz/¼ cup) caster sugar

❀ Melting method
❀ Cake tin: one 20 × 30 cm (8" × 12") tin, greased and floured
❀ Oven temperature: 180°C (350°F/Gas Mark 4)
❀ Baking time: 25 minutes

In a saucepan, melt the butter and stir in the molasses. Remove from the heat, add the milk and mix. Leave it to cool for a few minutes.

In a mixing bowl, sift the flour, salt, baking powder, bicarbonate of soda and ginger. Add the sugar and mix. Stir in the butter mixture.

Turn into the prepared cake tin and bake for 25 minutes. Remove from the oven and allow to cool for 10 minutes. Turn out onto a wire cooling rack. While still warm, cut into squares, diamonds or any shape required.

Spice Slice

VEGAN

50 g (2 oz/¼ cup) vegetable margarine or butter
2 tablespoons honey, agave syrup or golden syrup
2 tablespoons sunflower oil
50 g (2 oz/¼ cup) muscovado sugar
200 ml (7 fl oz/¾ cup) apple juice
100 g (3½ oz/¾ cup) self-raising wholemeal flour
100 g (3½ oz/¾ cup) self-raising flour
1 teaspoon baking powder
2 teaspoons mixed spice

❋ Topping:
50 g (2 oz/½ cup) oat flakes
2 tablespoons honey

❋ Creaming method
❋ Cake tin: one 20 × 30 cm (8" × 12") rectangular tin, greased and floured
❋ Oven temperature: 180°C (350°F/Gas Mark 4)
❋ Baking time: 25 minutes

In a mixing bowl, cream the margarine or butter, honey, oil and sugar together until light and fluffy. Mix in the apple juice, little by little. Sift in the flours, baking powder and spice and mix until well blended. Pour into the prepared cake tin.

Combine the oat flakes and honey and sprinkle the mixture over the cake. Bake for 25 minutes. Let the cake cool in the tin for 20 minutes and cut into squares.

Carrot Cake

VEGAN

100 g (3½ oz/¾ cup) raisins
150 g (5 oz/1 cup) grated carrots
150 ml (5 fl oz/⅔ cup) water
4 tablespoons honey, agave syrup or golden syrup
50 g (2 oz/¼ cup) butter or vegetable margarine
50 g (2 oz/¼ cup) muscovado sugar
200 g (7 oz/1½ cups) plain flour
1 tablespoon arrowroot or cornflour
½ teaspoon each ground nutmeg and cinnamon
2 teaspoons baking powder

❀ Melting method
❀ Cake tin: one 18 × 25 cm (7" × 10") rectangular tin, greased and floured
❀ Oven temperature: 180°C (350°F/Gas Mark 4)
❀ Baking time: 45–50 minutes

In a saucepan, boil the raisins and the grated carrot in the water for 5 minutes. Remove from the heat and mix in the honey, butter and sugar. Allow to cool.

In a mixing bowl, sift the flour, arrowroot, nutmeg, cinnamon and baking powder. Make a well in the centre and pour in the wet mixture. Beat with a spoon for one minute. Turn into the prepared cake tin and bake for 45 minutes. Check if the centre of the cake is dry. If it is not, leave for a few minutes longer.

Remove from the oven and allow to cool for 10 minutes. Turn out onto a wire cooling rack. When cold, cut into squares.

Old-fashioned Carrot Cake

VEGAN

150 ml (5 fl oz/⅔ cup) water
100 g (3½ oz/½ cup) muscovado sugar
100 g (3½ oz/¾ cup) raisins
½ teaspoon ground nutmeg
1 teaspoon ground cinnamon
½ teaspoon ground cloves
200 g (7 oz/1¼ cup) grated carrot
250 g (8 oz/2 cups) plain flour
2 teaspoons baking powder
1 teaspoon bicarbonate of soda
a pinch of salt
100 g (3½ oz/½ cup) chopped walnuts

❀ Melting method
❀ Cake tin: one 20 × 30 cm (8" × 12") rectangular tin or 1 kg (2 lb) loaf tin, greased and floured
❀ Oven temperature: 150°C (300°F/Gas Mark 3)
❀ Baking time: about 2 hours

If possible, start this mixture the night before. In a saucepan, boil the water, sugar, raisins, spices and the grated carrot for 5 minutes. Pour the mixture into a mixing bowl and leave it for at least 4 hours. Add the other ingredients and beat with a spoon. Turn into the prepared cake tin and bake for approximately 2 hours. Check the cake every 15 minutes after the first hour.

When it is ready, it should be deep brown and should leave the sides of the tin. Check with a skewer or cocktail stick. If it comes out clean, the cake is ready. Remove from the oven and allow to cool for 10 minutes. Turn out onto a wire cooling rack, and cut into squares or slices when cold.

Tahini Squares

VEGAN

300 g (10 oz/2½ cups) plain or wholemeal flour, or equal amounts of both
5 teaspoons baking powder
50 g (2 oz/¼ cup) raisins
50 g (2 oz/¼ cup) chopped mixed nuts
4 tablespoons sunflower oil
3 rounded tablespoons tahini
300 ml (10 fl oz/1¼ cups) fruit juice
150 g (5 oz/¾ cup) muscovado sugar

❁ Dry and wet method
❁ Cake tin: one 20 × 30 cm (8" × 12") rectangular tin, greased and floured
❁ Oven temperature: 190°C (375°F/Gas Mark 5)
❁ Baking time: 35–40 minutes

In a mixing bowl, sift the flour and the baking powder. Mix in the raisins and nuts. In a smaller mixing bowl or a measuring jug, mix the oil and tahini. Add the fruit juice and the sugar. Combine the dry and wet mixtures and beat with a spoon.

Turn into the prepared cake tin. Bake for 35 minutes. Check if the centre of the cake is dry. If it is not, leave the cake in the oven for a few minutes longer.

Remove from the oven and allow to cool for 10 minutes. Turn out onto a wire cooling rack. When cold, cut into squares.

Date Squares

VEGAN

100 g (3½ oz/¾ cup) dates
150 ml (5 fl oz/⅔ cup) water
150 g (5 oz/1¼ cups) flour
3 teaspoons baking powder
100 g (3½ oz/1 cup) porridge (rolled) oats
150 g (5 oz/¾ cup) butter or vegetable margarine
100 g (3½ oz/½ cup) caster sugar

❀ Rub-in method
❀ Cake tin: one 18 × 25 cm (7" × 10") rectangular tin, greased and floured
❀ Oven temperature: 180°C (350°F/Gas Mark 4)
❀ Baking time: 45–50 minutes

Chop the dates and boil them in the water for 5 minutes. Remove from the heat and allow to cool. In a mixing bowl, mix the flour, baking powder and porridge oats. Cut the butter into small cubes and mix it into the flour with your fingertips until the mixture resembles fine breadcrumbs. Add the sugar and mix well. Add the water in which the dates were boiled and stir.

Spoon half of the mixture into the prepared baking tin. Sprinkle on the chopped dates. Spoon the other half of the cake mixture on top. Bake for approximately 45 to 50 minutes.

Remove from the oven and allow to cool for 10 minutes. Turn out onto a wire cooling rack. When cold, cut into squares.

Charioteer Cake

VEGAN

50 g (2 oz/¼ cup) butter or vegetable margarine
100 ml (3½ fl oz/½ cup) molasses
150 g (5 oz/¾ cup) muscovado sugar
200 ml (7 fl oz/¾ cup) milk or soya milk
300 g (10 oz/2½ cups) flour
4 teaspoons baking powder
100 g (3½ oz/¾ cup) chopped mixed peel

❋ Melting method
❋ Cake tin: one 20 × 30 cm (8" × 12") rectangular tin, greased and floured
❋ Oven temperature: 180°C (350°F/Gas Mark 4)
❋ Baking time: 25–30 minutes

In a saucepan, melt the butter and mix in the molasses. Remove from the heat and add the sugar. Mix well and let cool. Mix in the milk.

In a mixing bowl, sift the flour and the baking powder. Mix in the chopped peel. Pour the wet mixture over the dry and beat with a spoon. Turn into the prepared cake tin and bake for 25 minutes. Check if the centre of the cake is dry. If it is not, leave the cake in the oven for a few minutes longer.

Remove from the oven and allow to cool for 10 minutes. Turn out onto a wire cooling rack. When cold, cut into squares.

Basler Leckerli

A spicy cake from Switzerland

VEGAN

250 g (8 oz/2 cups) plain flour
1 tablespoon cinnamon
¼ teaspoon nutmeg
1 teaspoon ground cloves
2 teaspoons baking powder
175 g (6 oz/1 cup) caster sugar
150 g (5 oz/¾ cup) chopped almonds
the finely grated rinds of 1 lemon and 1 orange
175 g (6 fl oz/¾ cup) molasses
50 ml (2 fl oz/¼ cup) yoghurt or soya yoghurt

❄ One-step method
❄ Cake tin: one 20 × 30 cm (8" × 12") rectangular tin, or two smaller ones, greased and floured
❄ Oven temperature: 180°C (350°F/Gas Mark 4) for 10 minutes, 160°C (325°F/Gas Mark 3) for 15 minutes
❄ Baking time: 25 minutes

Sift together the flour, spices and baking powder. Mix in the other ingredients except the yoghurt. Gradually add the yoghurt until the mixture has a sticky consistency. Dip your hands in warm water, then spread the mixture in the prepared tin. Prick the surface with a fork. Bake for 25 minutes.

Remove from the oven, and while the cake is still warm, cover it with a thin layer of Glacé Icing. Then cut into squares. This cake keeps well stored in an airtight tin.

Peach Squares

VEGAN

50 g (2 oz/¼ cup) soft butter or vegetable margarine
100 g (3½ oz/½ cup) caster sugar
1 tablespoon cornflour dissolved in 2 tablespoons of water
150 g (5 oz/1¼ cups) plain flour
3 teaspoons baking powder
240 ml (8 fl oz/1 cup) chopped peaches and a little juice

❁ Topping: 50 g (2 oz/¼ cup) butter or vegetable margarine
50 g (2 oz/¼ cup) caster sugar
¼ teaspoon each of ground cinnamon and ground nutmeg
100 g (3½ oz/1 cup) oat flakes

❁ Creaming method
❁ Cake tin: one 20 × 30 cm (8" × 12") rectangular tin, greased and floured
❁ Oven temperature: 180°C (350°F/Gas Mark 4)
❁ Baking time: 35 minutes

Prepare the topping first. In a saucepan, mix the butter or margarine, the sugar and the spices. Heat over a low flame until the mixture comes to a boil. Remove from the heat and mix in the oat flakes. Let it cool.

In a mixing bowl, beat the butter and the sugar. Mix in the dissolved cornflour. Sift the flour and the baking powder over the mixture and beat with a spoon. Stir in the chopped peaches. If the mixture is stiff or very dry, add a little more juice. Turn into the prepared cake tin. Sprinkle the topping over the mixture and bake for 35 minutes. Remove from the oven and allow to cool for 30 minutes. Cut into squares.

FRUIT LOAVES

AND

TEA BREADS

The cakes in this section are usually baked in bread tins. The tins should be greased with butter or vegetable margarine and sprinkled with flour. For some of the heavier fruit cakes, it is necessary to lightly grease and then line the tin with greaseproof paper.

Folar

A Traditional Portuguese Bread
<small>VEGAN</small>

300 ml (10 fl oz /1¼ cups) warm milk or soya milk
30 g (1 oz) fresh yeast
500 g (1 lb/4 cups) flour
a pinch of salt
50 g (2 oz/¼ cup) sugar
200 g (7 oz/1 cup) butter or vegetable margarine, melted
1 teaspoon ground fennel seeds
1 teaspoon ground cinnamon
150 g (5 oz) Marzipan
a little milk or soya milk for brushing

❀ Bread-making method
❀ Rising and proving time: 2½ hours
❀ Cake tin: one baking sheet, greased with butter
❀ Oven temperature: 190°C (375°F/Gas Mark 5)
❀ Baking time: 25–30 minutes

Heat the milk till just warm to the finger. Add the yeast and dissolve it by crumbling it with fingertips. Mix in 1 tablespoon flour. Cover with a clean tea towel and leave the mixture for 10 minutes or until bubbles start to appear on the surface.

Sift the rest of the flour and the salt in a mixing bowl, make a well in the centre and pour in the milk mixture. Add the sugar and mix well. Turn the mixture onto a floured surface and knead for 10 minutes. Add the melted butter and spices. Knead for another 5 minutes until the dough is light and firm. Place in a greased bowl, cover with a clean cloth and leave for about two hours or until doubled in size.

In the meantime, prepare the marzipan. Divide it into 4 parts and form each into an oval. Knead the dough for one minute and shape it into a round, approximately 17 to 20 cm (7" to 8") in diameter.

Place the four "eggs" on the dough to form a cross and press them lightly into the dough. Brush the whole surface with a little milk. Allow to prove for 30 minutes and then bake in a hot oven for approximately 25 to 30 minutes until golden brown.

Peanut Butter Cake

Vegan

4 tablespoons peanut butter
100 g (3½ oz/½ cup) muscovado sugar
75 ml (2½ fl oz/⅓ cup) yoghurt or soya yoghurt
200 g (7 oz/1½ cups) self-raising flour
1 teaspoon baking powder
100 ml (3½ fl oz/½ cup) milk or soya milk

❋ One-step method
❋ Cake tin: one 1 kg (2 lb) loaf tin, greased and floured
❋ Oven temperature: 180°C (350°F/Gas Mark 4)
❋ Baking time: 30–35 minutes

In a mixing bowl, mix together the peanut butter and the sugar. Mix in the yoghurt. Sift the flour and baking powder on top of the mixture. Add the milk gradually, and beat with a spoon.

Turn into the prepared tin and bake for 30 minutes. Check if the centre of the cake is dry. If it is not, leave in the oven for another 5 minutes. Let the cake cool in the tin for about 10 minutes, then turn out and cool completely on a wire rack.

Walnut Malt Loaf

Vegan

150 g (5 oz/1¼ cups) wholemeal flour
100 g (3½ oz/¾ cup) self-raising flour
1 teaspoon baking powder
½ teaspoon nutmeg
100 g (3½ oz/¾ cup) sultanas
50 g (2 oz/¼ cup) chopped walnuts
100 g (3½ oz/½ cup) muscovado sugar
200 g (7 oz/¾ cup) malt extract
200 ml (7 fl oz/¾ cup) milk or soya milk

❁ Dry and wet method
❁ Cake tin: one 1 kg (2 lb) loaf tin, or two ½ kg (1 lb) loaf tins, greased and lined with greaseproof paper
❁ Oven temperature: 170°C (340°F/Gas Mark 3)
❁ Baking time: 60 minutes

Sift the flours, baking powder and nutmeg into a bowl. Stir in the sultanas, walnuts and sugar.

Pour the malt extract into a saucepan and heat it over low heat until it is liquid. Add the milk and stir. Pour this mixture into the dry ingredients and mix well.

Spoon the mixture into the tin and bake for 60 minutes or until firm and still sticky but dry. Remove from the oven and leave to cool in the tin for 15 minutes. Turn onto a wire tray to cool.

Serve sliced and buttered.

Cherry Cake

VEGAN

150 g (5 oz/1¼ cups) plain flour
2 teaspoons baking powder
100 g (3½ oz/½ cup) caster sugar
50 g (2 oz/¼ cup) semolina
50 g (2 oz/¼ cup) chopped glacé cherries
3 tablespoons milk or soya milk
75 ml (2½ fl oz/⅓ cup) yoghurt or soya yoghurt
½ teaspoon vanilla essence
4 tablespoons sunflower oil

❀ One-step method
❀ Cake tin: one ½ kg (1 lb) loaf tin, greased and floured
❀ Oven temperature: 180°C (350°F/Gas Mark 4)
❀ Baking time: 30–35 minutes

In a mixing bowl, sift the flour and baking powder. Add the sugar, semolina and cherries. Mix in the milk, yoghurt, vanilla and oil.

Spoon into the prepared loaf tin. Bake the cake for 30 minutes. Check if the centre of the cake is dry. If it is not, leave in the oven for another 5 minutes. Let the cake cool in the tin for about 10 minutes, then turn out and cool completely on a wire rack.

Afternoon Tea Cake

Vegan

150 g (5 oz/1¼ cups) plain flour
50 g (2 oz/½ cup) carob powder
2 teaspoons baking powder
150 ml (5 fl oz/⅔ cup) cold water
½ tablespoon lemon juice
4 tablespoons sunflower oil
½ teaspoon vanilla essence
100 g (3½ oz/½ cup) muscovado sugar

❀ Dry and wet method
❀ Cake tin: one ½ kg (1 lb) loaf tin, greased and floured
❀ Oven temperature: 180°C (350°F/Gas Mark 4)
❀ Baking time: 30–35 minutes

In a mixing bowl, sift the flour, carob powder and baking powder.

In a measuring jug, mix the water, lemon juice, oil, vanilla and sugar. Combine the two mixtures and beat for one minute with a spoon.

Turn into the prepared loaf tin. Bake for 30 minutes. Check if the centre of the cake is dry. If it is not, leave in the oven for another 5 minutes. Let the cake cool in the tin for about 10 minutes, then turn out and cool completely on a wire rack.

Traditional Panetone

An Italian Christmas Bread
VEGAN

300 ml (3½ fl oz/½ cup) warm water
30 g (1 oz) fresh yeast
300 g (10 oz/2½ cups) strong bread flour
100 g (3½ oz/½ cup) sugar
75 ml (2½ fl oz/⅓ cup) yoghurt or soya yoghurt
1 teaspoon salt
100 g (3½ oz/¾ cup) raisins
100 g (3½ oz/¾ cup) chopped mixed peel
1 tablespoon grated lemon rind
1 teaspoon vanilla essence
100 g (3½ oz/½ cup) soft butter or vegetable margarine

❀ Bread-making method
❀ Proving time: 3 hours
❀ Cake tin: a 15 cm (6") deep round tin, greased and lined with greaseproof paper
❀ Oven temperature: 220°C (425°F/Gas Mark 7) for 10 minutes, then 180°C (350°F/Gas Mark 4) for 30 minutes
❀ Baking time: 40 minutes

Heat the water till just warm to the finger. Add the yeast and dissolve it by crumbling it with fingertips. Mix in 1 tablespoon flour. Cover mixture with a tea towel and leave it for 10 minutes or until bubbles start to appear on the surface.

Mix in all the other ingredients except the butter. If the mixture is too wet, add a little more flour. Turn onto a floured surface and knead for 10 minutes. While kneading, add the softened butter, a little at a time.

Turn the mixture into the prepared tin. Cover with a tea towel and prove for three hours in a draft-free place. Bake in a hot oven (220°C) for 10 minutes. Lower the heat to 180°C and bake for another 30 minutes, until the top is golden brown.

Orange Tea Bread

VEGAN

150 ml (5 fl oz/⅔ cup) yoghurt or soya yoghurt
the juice and the finely grated rind of 1 medium orange
100 g (3½ oz/½ cup) caster sugar
75 ml (2½ fl oz/⅔ cup) sunflower oil
100 g (3½ oz/½ cup) orange marmalade
250 g (8 oz/2 cups) plain flour
50 g (2 oz/½ cup) cornflour
5 teaspoons baking powder

❀ One-step method
❀ Cake tin: one 1 kg (2 lb) loaf tin, greased and floured
❀ Oven temperature: 180°C (350°F/Gas Mark 4)
❀ Baking time: 30–35 minutes

In a mixing bowl, mix the yoghurt, orange juice and rind, sugar, oil and marmalade. Sift the flour, cornflour and baking powder on top and mix with a spoon.

Bake the cake for 30 minutes. Check if the centre of the cake is dry. If it is not, leave the cake in the oven for another 5 minutes. Let it cool in the tin for about 10 minutes, then turn out and cool on a wire rack.

Nutmeg Cake

50 ml (2 fl oz/¼ cup) milk
the juice of half a lemon
100 ml (3½ fl oz/½ cup) water
100 ml (3½ fl oz/½ cup) honey
50 g (2 oz/2 tablespoons) caster sugar
50 g (2 oz/2 tablespoons) vegetable margarine
150 g (5 oz/1¼ cups) plain flour
4 teaspoons baking powder
50 g (2 oz/½ cup) cornflour
50 g (2 oz/½ cup) dry powdered milk
1 teaspoon ground nutmeg
25 g (1 oz/2 tablespoons) carob powder

❀ Creaming method
❀ Cake tin: one 1 kg (2 lb) loaf tin, greased and floured
❀ Oven temperature: 180°C (350°F/Gas Mark 4)
❀ Baking time: 30–35 minutes

Mix the milk with the lemon juice and leave for a few minutes until the milk curdles. Mix in the water and the honey.

In a mixing bowl, beat the sugar and the margarine until light and fluffy. Mix in the curdled milk.

Sift together the flour, baking powder, cornflour, powdered milk, nutmeg and carob powder, and add them to the wet mixture.

Turn into the prepared loaf tin. Bake the cake for 30 minutes. Check if the centre of the cake is dry. If it is not, leave in the oven for another 5 minutes. Let the cake cool in the tin for about 10 minutes, then turn out and cool completely on a wire rack.

Fig Cake

VEGAN

150 g (5 oz/1 cup) dry figs, chopped
3 tablespoons milk or soya milk
100 g (3½ oz/½ cup) muscovado sugar
100 ml (3½ fl oz/½ cup) yoghurt or soya yoghurt
6 tablespoons sunflower oil
100 g (3½ oz/¾ cup) plain flour
100 g (3½ oz/¾ cup) wholemeal flour
4 teaspoons baking powder

❀ One-step method
❀ Cake tin: one 1 kg (2 lb) loaf tin, greased and floured
❀ Oven temperature: 180°C (350°F/Gas Mark 4)
❀ Baking time: 30–35 minutes

Soak the figs in hot water for about one hour. Discard the water and chop the figs.

In a mixing bowl, beat the milk with the sugar. Add the yoghurt and the oil and mix. Sift the flours and the baking powder and mix well. Mix in the figs.

Turn into the prepared loaf tin. Bake the cake for 30 minutes. Check if the centre of the cake is dry. If it is not, leave in the oven for another 5 minutes. Let the cake cool in the tin for about 10 minutes, then turn out and cool completely on a wire rack.

Quick Fruit Cake

VEGAN

150 g (5 oz/1 cup) mixed dried fruit: raisins, sultanas, currants, figs, dates, bananas, etc.
   (chop the larger fruits)
200 ml (7 fl oz/¾ cup) water
100 g (3½ oz/½ cup) muscovado sugar
2 teaspoons mixed spice
3 tablespoons butter or vegetable margarine
200 g (7 oz/1½ cups) plain flour
1 teaspoon bicarbonate of soda
2 teaspoons baking powder

❀ Melting method
❀ Cake tin: one 1 kg (2 lb) loaf tin, greased and floured
❀ Oven temperature: 180°C (350°F/Gas Mark 4)
❀ Baking time: 40–45 minutes

Place the fruit, water, sugar and spice in a saucepan and boil for 5 minutes. Remove from the heat and mix in the butter. Let the mixture cool a little.

In the meantime, in a mixing bowl, sift the flour, bicarbonate of soda and baking powder. When the fruit mixture is nearly cold, combine the two mixtures and beat with a spoon.

Turn into the prepared loaf tin. Bake for 40–45 minutes or until the centre of the cake is dry. Remove from the oven and let the cake cool for about 10 minutes. Turn out and cool completely on a wire rack.

Molasses Fruit Cake

VEGAN

This is a delicious, sticky cake which should be served cut into thin slices. It can be stored in an airtight tin for up to two weeks.

900 g (2 lb/7 cups) mixed dried fruit: raisins, sultanas, currants, figs, dates, bananas, etc. (chop the larger fruits)
300 ml (10 fl oz/1¼ cups) boiling water
100 ml (3½ fl oz/½ cup) sunflower oil
2 tablespoons molasses
300 g (10 oz/2½ cups) plain flour
4 teaspoons mixed spice
5 teaspoons baking powder

❁ Dry and wet method
❁ Cake tin: two 1 kg (2 lb) loaf tins or one 20 cm (8") round tin, greased and lined with greaseproof paper
❁ Oven temperature: 160°C (325°F/Gas Mark 3)
❁ Baking time: 60–65 minutes

Soak the fruit in the boiling water while you prepare the cake tin and the rest of the batter. Add the oil and the molasses and mix until the molasses has dissolved. Let it cool.

In a mixing bowl, sift the flour, spice and baking powder. When the wet mixture has cooled, combine the two mixtures and beat with a spoon.

Spoon into the loaf tin and bake the cake for about 60 minutes. Check if the centre of the cake is dry. If it is not, leave in the oven for another 5 minutes. After removing it from the oven, let it stand for 10 minutes, then turn out and remove the paper. Cool on a wire rack.

Apple Crumble Cake

Vegan

150 g (5 oz/1¼ cups) self-raising flour
50 g (2 oz/½ cup) soft brown sugar
50 g (2 oz/¼ cup) ground almonds
50 g (2 oz/¼ cup) butter or vegetable margarine
2 teaspoons lemon juice
2 tablespoons milk or soya milk

❀ Filling: ½ kg (1 lb) apples
100 g (3½ oz/½ cup) caster sugar
1 tablespoon lemon juice

❀ Topping: 100 g (3½ oz/¾ cup) self-raising flour
50 g (2 oz/2 tablespoons) sugar
1 teaspoon cinnamon
50 g (2 oz/2 tablespoons) butter or vegetable margarine

❀ Rub-in method
❀ Cake tin: one 20 cm (8") round tin, preferably with a spring clip, greased and floured
❀ Oven temperature: 180°C (350°F/Gas Mark 4)
❀ Baking time: 60–70 minutes

Sift together the flour, sugar and almonds. Rub in the butter until the mixture resembles fine breadcrumbs. Mix in the lemon juice and the milk to form a firm dough. Press the dough into the tin. Peel and slice the apples. Mix them with the sugar and lemon juice and place them on top of the mixture in the tin.

For the topping, sift the flour, sugar and cinnamon. Rub in the butter until the mixture resembles fine breadcrumbs. Spoon the crumbs over the apples. Bake for 60 to 70 minutes.

Cherry Loaf

VEGAN

150 g (5 oz/1¼ cups) self-raising flour
1 teaspoon ground ginger
50 g (2 oz/¼ cup) caster sugar
50 g (2 oz/¼ cup) glacé cherries, chopped
3 tablespoons sunflower oil
4 tablespoons honey or golden syrup
100 ml (3½ fl oz/½ cup) milk or soya milk

❀ One-step method
❀ Cake tin: one ½ kg (1 lb) loaf tin, greased and floured
❀ Oven temperature: 180°C (350°F/Gas Mark 4)
❀ Baking time: 40–45 minutes

Sift the dry ingredients and stir in the cherries. Add all the other ingredients and mix well. Spoon the mixture into the prepared tin and bake for 40 minutes. Check if the centre of the cake is dry. If it is not, leave in the oven for another 5 minutes. Let the cake cool for about 10 minutes, then turn out and cool completely on a wire rack.

Apple and Date Cake

2 small apples
50 g (2 oz/¼ cup) muscovado sugar
1 tablespoon honey
150 g (5 oz/1¼ cups) plain flour
3 teaspoons baking powder
50 g (2 oz/¼ cup) dates, chopped
3 tablespoons powdered milk
2 tablespoons water

❀ Creaming method
❀ Cake tin: one 500 g (1 lb) loaf tin, greased and floured
❀ Oven temperature: 190°C (375°F/Gas Mark 5)
❀ Baking time: 30–35 minutes

Peel and chop the apples. Cook them over very low heat until soft. Remove from the heat, mix in the sugar and the honey. Leave to cool.

In a mixing bowl, sift the flour and the baking powder. Mix in the dates and the powdered milk. Add the apples and water. Beat with a spoon.

Spoon the mixture into the prepared tin and bake for 30 minutes. Check if the centre of the cake is dry. If it is not, leave in the oven for another 5 minutes. Let the cake cool for about 10 minutes, then turn out and cool completely on a wire rack.

Marble Cake

3 tablespoons cornflour
3 tablespoons cold milk or soya milk
50 g (2 oz/¼ cup) butter or vegetable margarine
100 g (3½ oz/½ cup) caster sugar
1 teaspoon vanilla essence
100 ml (3½ fl oz/½ cup) yoghurt or soya yoghurt
200 g (7 oz/1½ cups) plain flour
3 teaspoons baking powder
1 tablespoon carob powder dissolved in 2 tablespoons boiling water

❈ Creaming method
❈ Cake tin: one 1 kg (2 lb) loaf tin or one ring cake tin, greased and floured
❈ Oven temperature: 180°C (350°F/Gas Mark 4)
❈ Baking time: 30–35 minutes

In a cup, dissolve the cornflour in the cold milk. In a mixing bowl, beat the butter with the sugar until light and fluffy. Gradually, add the cornflour mixture and the vanilla. Mix in the yoghurt. Sift the flour and the baking powder on top and beat for one minute.

Spoon half of the mixture into the prepared tin. Add the dissolved carob to the other half and mix well. Spoon the rest of the mixture into the tin. Carefully swirl the mixture with a knife or a spoon handle, to give a marble effect.

Bake for 30 minutes. Check if the centre of the cake is dry. If it is not, leave in the oven for another 5 minutes. Let the cake cool for about 10 minutes, then turn out and cool completely on a wire rack.

Honey Cake

100 ml (3½ fl oz/½ cup) milk
200 ml (7 fl oz/¾ cup) honey
125 ml (4 fl oz/½ cup) yoghurt
2 tablespoons sunflower oil
100 g (3½ oz/½ cup) caster sugar
100 g (3½ oz/¾ cup) wholemeal flour
200 g (7 oz/1½ cups) plain flour
5 teaspoons baking powder

❀ Dry and wet method
❀ Cake tin: one 20 cm (8") round cake tin, greased and floured
❀ Oven temperature: 180°C (350°F/Gas Mark 4)
❀ Baking time: 30–35 minutes

In a saucepan, heat the milk until lukewarm. Remove from the heat and mix in the honey. Add the yoghurt, oil and sugar. In a mixing bowl, sift the flours and the baking powder. Combine the two mixtures and beat with a spoon.

Bake for 30 minutes. Check if the centre of the cake is dry. If it is not, leave in the oven for another 5 minutes. Let the cake cool for about 10 minutes, then turn out and cool completely on a wire rack.

Walnut Cake

25 g (1 oz/2 tablespoons) butter or vegetable margarine
75 ml (2½ fl oz/⅓ cup) honey
100 ml (3½ fl oz/½ cup) milk
50 ml (2 fl oz/¼ cup) yoghurt
50 g (2 oz/¼ cup) muscovado sugar
200 g (7 oz/1½ cups) plain flour
3 teaspoons baking powder
50 g (2 oz/¼ cup) chopped walnuts

❋ Melting method
❋ Cake tin: one 1 kg (2 lb) loaf tin, greased and floured
❋ Oven temperature: 180°C (350°F/Gas Mark 4)
❋ Baking time: 35–40 minutes

In a saucepan, melt the butter. Remove from the heat and stir in the honey. In a mixing bowl, mix the milk with the yoghurt. Mix in the sugar. Sift the flour and baking powder over the milk and blend together. Add the butter and the honey. Beat with a spoon. Finally, stir in the walnuts.

Turn into the prepared tin and bake for 35 to 40 minutes. Check if the centre of the cake is dry. If it is not, leave in the oven for another 5 minutes. Let the cake cool for about 10 minutes, then turn out and cool completely on a wire rack.

Easter Simnel Cake

Vegan

600 g (1 lb/21 oz) Marzipan
500 g (1 lb/3 cups) mixed dried fruit: raisins, sultanas, currants and chopped peel
100 ml (3½ fl oz/½ cup) water
100 g (3½ oz/½ cup) muscovado sugar
2 teaspoons mixed spice
3 tablespoons butter or vegetable margarine
the juice and grated rind of 1 large orange
200 g (7 oz/1½ cups) plain flour
4 teaspoons baking powder
2 tablespoons apricot jam or honey

❀ Melting method
❀ Cake tin: one 18 cm (7") round tin, greased and lined with greaseproof paper
❀ Oven temperature: 160°C (325°F/Gas Mark 3)
❀ Baking time: 50–60 minutes

Prepare a double quantity of Marzipan, wrap in cling film and keep in a cool, dry place. Place the fruit, water, sugar and spice in a saucepan and boil for 5 minutes. Remove from the heat and mix in the butter or margarine. Let the mixture cool a little and add the orange juice and rind.

In the meantime, in a mixing bowl, sift together the flour and the baking powder. When the fruit mixture is nearly cold, combine the two mixtures and beat with a spoon.

Spoon half of the mixture into the prepared cake tin. Divide the marzipan into three equal amounts. Roll out or pat one part smoothly into an 18 cm (7") circle, and place it on top of the cake mixture in the tin. Cover with the rest of the cake mixture, spreading it evenly with the back of a spoon.

Bake the cake for 50 to 60 minutes. Check if the centre of the cake is dry. If it is not, leave in the oven for another 5 minutes. Let the cake cool for about 10 minutes, then turn out and remove the greaseproof paper. Cool completely on a wire rack.

When cold, brush the top of the cake with sieved jam or honey. Roll out another third of the marzipan into an 18 cm (7") circle and place it on top of the cake. Shape the rest of the Marzipan into 12 balls. Arrange them round the edge of the cake. Brush with a little honey and place under a hot grill for a few minutes until the balls are lightly browned.

Stollen

VEGAN

A rich yeasted cake from Germany served especially at Christmas.

450 g (1 lb/3 cups) flour
½ teaspoon salt
200 ml (7 fl oz/¾ cup) warm milk or soya milk
30 g (1 oz) fresh yeast
100 g (3½ oz/½ cup) butter or vegetable margarine
50 g (2 oz/¼ cup) sugar
1 tablespoon lemon juice
200 g (7 oz/1¼ cups) raisins
50 g (2 oz/¼ cup) chopped walnuts
50 g (2 oz/¼ cup) glacé cherries, chopped
50 g (2 oz/¼ cup) chopped mixed peel
150 g (5 oz) Marzipan
1 quantity Glacé Icing
50 g (2 oz/⅓ cup) chopped mixed peel and chopped cherries for decoration

❋ Bread-making method
❋ Rising and proving time: 1 hour plus 30 minutes
❋ Cake tin: one large rectangular tin, 20 × 30 cm (8" × 12"), greased
❋ Oven temperature: 190°C (375°F/Gas Mark 5)
❋ Baking time: 35 minutes

Sift the flour and the salt in a mixing bowl and place in a warm oven for 10 minutes. Heat the milk till just warm to the finger. Add the yeast and dissolve it by crumbling it with your fingertips. Mix in 1 tablespoon flour. Cover with a tea towel and set aside for 10 minutes or until bubbles start to appear on the surface. Stir in the butter, sugar and lemon juice.

Add the warm flour and beat with a spoon until the mixture no longer sticks to the sides of the bowl. Add the raisins, walnuts, cherries and peel. Turn onto a floured surface and knead for 5 minutes. Place the dough in an oiled mixing bowl, cover with a tea towel and leave for approximately 1 hour.

In the meantime, prepare the Marzipan and roll it into a cylinder about 30 cm (12") long.

When the dough has doubled in size, turn it onto a floured surface and knead for 1 minute. Roll it out to about 30 cm × 12 cm (12" × 5").

Place the Marzipan in the middle and roll the dough around it. Place the loaf carefully on the prepared tin and cover with a damp, warm tea towel. Leave it to prove for 30 minutes in a corner free of drafts. Bake for 35 minutes.

Leave the bread to cool for 5 minutes and remove from the tin. Prepare the icing and spread it over the loaf. Decorate with the chopped peel and cherries.

Tutti Frutti Cake

Vegan

150 ml (5 fl oz/⅔ cup) water
1 large carrot, grated
2 teaspoons mixed spice
50 g (2 oz/¼ cup) raisins
50 g (2 oz/¼ cup) dates, chopped
50 g (2 oz/¼ cup) prunes or dried bananas, chopped
50 g (2 oz/¼ cup) chopped mixed peel
50 ml (2 fl oz/¼ cup) honey or molasses
4 tablespoons sunflower oil
200 g (7 oz/1½ cups) flour
4 teaspoons baking powder

❁ Dry and wet method
❁ Cake tin: one 1 kg (2 lb) loaf tin, greased and floured
❁ Oven temperature: 180°C (350°F/Gas Mark 4)
❁ Baking time: 45–50 minutes

In a saucepan, heat the water and add the grated carrot, spice and fruit. Bring to a boil, lower the heat and cook for 5 minutes. Remove the saucepan from the heat and mix in the molasses or honey and the oil. Allow the mixture to cool.

In a mixing bowl, sift the flour and the baking powder. Combine the dry and wet mixtures and beat with a spoon.

Turn into the prepared tin and bake for 45 minutes. Check if the centre of the cake is dry. If it is not, leave in the oven for another 5 minutes. Let the cake cool for about 10 minutes, then turn out and cool completely on a wire rack.

Seed Cake

Vegan

200 g (7 oz/1½ cups) plain flour
2 teaspoons baking powder
1 teaspoon bicarbonate of soda
50 g (2 oz/¼ cup) butter or vegetable margarine
100 g (3½ oz/½ cup) caster sugar
½ teaspoon caraway seeds
2 tablespoons poppy seeds
2 tablespoons sesame seeds
150 ml (5 fl oz/⅔ cup) milk or soya milk
1 tablespoon lemon juice
50 ml (2 fl oz/¼ cup) yoghurt or soya yoghurt

❊ Rub-in method
❊ Cake tin: one 1 kg (2 lb) loaf tin, greased and floured
❊ Oven temperature: 180°C (350°F/Gas Mark 4)
❊ Baking time: 30–35 minutes

Sift the flour, baking powder and bicarbonate of soda into a bowl. Cut the butter into small pieces and rub into the flour with your fingertips until the mixture resembles fine breadcrumbs. Mix in the sugar.

Add all the seeds and mix well. Make a well in the middle and pour in the milk, lemon juice and yoghurt. Beat with a spoon.

Turn into the prepared tin and bake for 30 minutes. Check if the centre of the cake is dry. If it is not, leave in the oven for another 5 minutes. Let the cake cool for about 10 minutes, then turn out and cool completely on a wire rack.

Banana and Walnut Cake

Vegan

150 g (5 oz/1¼ cups) plain flour
1½ teaspoons baking powder
100 ml (3½ fl oz/½ cup) yoghurt or soya yoghurt
2 bananas, mashed
50 g (2 oz/¼ cup) chopped walnuts
½ teaspoon vanilla essence
a pinch of ground nutmeg
50 g (2 oz/¼ cup) muscovado sugar
50 g (2 oz/¼ cup) vegetable margarine or butter

❀ Creaming method
❀ Cake tin: one 1 kg (2 lb) loaf tin, greased and floured
❀ Oven temperature: 180°C (350°F/Gas Mark 4)
❀ Baking time: 30–35 minutes

In a mixing bowl, sift the flour and baking powder. In a separate bowl, combine the yoghurt, mashed bananas, walnuts, vanilla and nutmeg.

In another bowl, break up the sugar, if using muscovado. Add the butter and beat until light and fluffy. Gradually stir together the yoghurt mixture with the creamed butter mixture, one spoonful at a time.

Spread the mixture into the prepared loaf tin. Bake for 30 minutes. Check if the centre of the cake is dry. If it is not, leave in the oven for another 5 minutes. Remove from the oven and allow to cool for 10 minutes, then turn out. Cut into slices when cold.

Potato Cake

VEGAN

80 ml (3 fl oz/⅓ cup) sunflower oil
100 g (3½ oz/½ cup) muscovado sugar
½ teaspoon vanilla essence
150 ml (5 fl oz/⅔ cup) yoghurt or soya yoghurt
100 g (3½ oz/¾ cup) plain flour
100 g (3½ oz/¾ cup) potato flour
4 teaspoons baking powder

❀ One-step method
❀ Cake tin: one 1 kg (2 lb) loaf tin, greased and floured
❀ Oven temperature: 180°C (350°F/Gas Mark 4)
❀ Baking time: 35–40 minutes

In a mixing bowl, combine the oil with the sugar, vanilla and yoghurt. Mix in the flour, the potato flour and the baking powder.

Spoon into the prepared loaf tin. Bake the cake for 35 minutes. Check if the centre of the cake is dry. If it is not, leave in the oven for another 5 minutes.

Let the cake cool for about 10 minutes, then turn out and cool completely on a wire rack. Cut the cake into slices and serve buttered or spread with jam.

Continental Sweet Loaf

VEGAN

200 ml (7 fl oz/¾ cup) warm milk or soya milk
30 g (1 oz) fresh yeast
300 g (10 oz/2½ cups) flour
50 g (2 oz/¼ cup) butter or vegetable margarine
200 g (7 oz/1¼ cups) mixed dried fruit: raisins, sultanas, currants, bananas, etc. (chop the larger fruits)
100 g (3½ oz/½ cup) sugar
a pinch of salt
50 g (2 oz/¼ cup) semolina
the finely grated rinds of 1 lemon and 1 orange

❀ Bread-making method
❀ Proving time: 60 minutes
❀ Cake tin: one 20 cm (8") round tin or two 1 kg (2 lb) loaf tins, greased and floured
❀ Oven temperature: 220°C (425°F/Gas Mark 7) for 10 minutes, and 180° C (350° F/ Gas Mark 4) for 35 minutes
❀ Baking time: 45 minutes

Heat the milk till just warm to the finger. Add the yeast and dissolve it by crumbling it with your fingertips. Mix in 1 tablespoon of flour. Cover with a tea towel and leave it for 10 minutes or until bubbles start to appear on the surface.

In a mixing bowl, cut the butter into the flour and rub it in until the mixture resembles fine breadcrumbs. Mix in the fruit, sugar, salt, semolina and grated rind. Make a well in the centre and pour in the yeast mixture. Beat with a spoon for two minutes.

Turn the mixture into the prepared tin. Cover with a tea towel and prove for 1 hour in a corner free from drafts. Bake in a hot oven (220°C) for 10 minutes. Lower the heat to 180°C and bake for another 35 minutes, or until the top is golden brown. When cold, ice with Glacé Icing.

Boiled Cake

VEGAN

150 g (5 oz/1¼ cups) plain flour
1 teaspoon bicarbonate of soda
a pinch of salt
½ teaspoon ground cinnamon
½ teaspoon ground cloves
1 teaspoon grated fresh ginger
100 ml (3½ fl oz/½ cup) molasses
200 ml (7 fl oz/¾ cup) milk or soya milk
100 g (3½ oz/¾ cup) dried fruit: sultanas, raisins, currants, chopped dates, bananas, etc. (chop the larger fruits)

❀ Dry and wet method
❀ Cake tin: one ½ litre (1 lb) pudding dish, greased with butter
❀ Steaming time: approximately 2 hours

In a mixing bowl, sift the flour, bicarbonate of soda, salt and ground spices. Mix in the ginger.

Heat the molasses until liquid. Remove from the heat and stir in the milk or soya milk. Combine the two mixtures, add the fruit and beat with a spoon for two minutes.

Turn into the prepared dish and steam in a covered saucepan of gently boiling water for approximately 2 hours, over low heat. Check that the saucepan does not go dry. Allow the cake to cool before turning out.

Saffron Tea Bread

VEGAN

300 ml (10 fl oz/1¼ cups) warm milk or soya milk
½ level teaspoon saffron strands
150 ml (5 fl oz/⅔ cup) warm water
15 g (½ oz) fresh yeast or the equivalent dried yeast
500 g (1 lb 2 oz/4 cups) plain flour
4 tablespoons butter or vegetable margarine
a pinch of salt
50 g (2 oz/¼ cup) sugar
100 g (3½ oz/¾ cup) raisins
100 g (3½ oz/¾ cup) chopped mixed peel

✿ Bread-making method
✿ Proving time: 1 hour
✿ Cake tin: one 20 cm (8") round tin or two 1 kg (2 lb) loaf tins, greased and floured
✿ Oven temperature: 220°C (425°F/Gas Mark 7) for 10 minutes, and 180°C (350°F/Gas Mark 4) for 30 minutes
✿ Baking time: 40 minutes

Boil the milk. Carefully dissolve the saffron in it. Allow to cool. Heat the water till just warm to the finger. Add the yeast and dissolve it by crumbling it between your fingertips. Mix in 1 tablespoon of flour. Cover with a tea towel and leave for 10 minutes.

In a mixing bowl, cut the butter into the flour and rub it in until the mixture resembles fine breadcrumbs. Mix in the salt, sugar, raisins and mixed peel. Combine the three mixtures and beat with a spoon.

Turn the mixture into the prepared tin. Cover with a tea towel and prove for at least 1 hour. Bake the cake in a hot oven (220°C) for 10 minutes. Lower the heat to 180°C and bake for another 30 minutes, or until the top of the cake is golden brown.

Brazilian Cake

VEGAN

the juice of 1 small lemon
100 ml (3½ fl oz/½ cup) milk or soya milk
50 g (2 oz/¼ cup) butter or vegetable margarine
100 g (3½ oz/½ cup) caster sugar
100 ml (3½ fl oz/½ cup) yoghurt or soya yoghurt
100 g (3½ oz/1 cup) cornflour
100 g (3½ oz/½ cup) maize or polenta flour
4 teaspoons baking powder

❋ Creaming method
❋ Cake tin: one 1 kg (2 lb) loaf tin, greased and floured
❋ Oven temperature: 180°C (350°F/Gas Mark 4)
❋ Baking time: 30–35 minutes

In a small bowl, mix the lemon juice with the milk. Leave aside until the milk curdles.

In a mixing bowl, beat the butter with the sugar until light and fluffy. Add the yoghurt and the curdled milk. Beat with a spoon. Mix in the cornflour, maize flour and baking powder.

Spoon into the prepared cake tin. Bake for 30 minutes. Check if the centre of the cake is dry. If it is not, leave in the oven for another 5 minutes.

Let the cake cool for about 10 minutes, then turn out and cool completely on a wire rack.

Bara Brith

VEGAN

This is a delicious, rich fruit bread from Wales. It can be served at room temperature at any time or toasted on cold days.

100 g (3½ oz/¾ cup) currants
50 g (2 oz/¼ cup) raisins
300 ml (10 fl oz/1¼ cups) milk or soya milk
50 g (2 oz/¼ cup) butter or vegetable margarine
30 g (1 oz) fresh yeast, or an equivalent amount of dried yeast
25 g (1 oz/2 tablespoons) chopped mixed peel
450 g (1 lb/3½ cups) plain flour, or equal amounts of plain and wholewheat flour
2 teaspoons mixed spice
1 teaspoon salt
50 g (2 oz/½ cup) soft brown sugar

✽ Bread-making method
✽ Rising time: 1 hour
✽ Cake tin: one 1 kg (2 lb) loaf tin, greased
✽ Oven temperature: 200°C (400°F/Gas Mark 6)
✽ Baking time: 30–35 minutes

Soak the dried fruit in the milk overnight in the refrigerator. Drain and reserve the milk.

Heat the butter and milk until the butter has melted. Allow to cool till just warm to the finger. Dissolve the yeast in the mixture. In a warm bowl, mix the fruit, peel, flour, spice, salt and sugar. Stir in the milk. Add a little more flour if the dough is too sticky. Knead on a floured surface for 5 minutes.

Shape the dough to fit into the prepared tin. Cover and let rise for 1 hour. Bake on the middle shelf of the oven for 30–35 minutes or until a skewer inserted into the centre comes out dry.

Allow to cool completely before cutting into slices. Store in an airtight tin.

Hazelnut Cake

Vegan

200 g (7 oz/1½ cups) plain flour
100 g (3½ oz/½ cup) caster sugar
4 teaspoons baking powder
100 g (3½ oz/½ cup) chopped hazelnuts
200 ml (7 fl oz/¾ cup) milk or soya milk
½ teaspoon vanilla essence
½ teaspoon almond essence
1 teaspoon grated lemon rind
5 tablespoons sunflower oil

❉ Dry and wet method
❉ Cake tin: one 1 kg (2 lb) loaf tin, greased and floured
❉ Oven temperature: 180°C (350°F/Gas Mark 4)
❉ Baking time: 40–45 minutes

In a mixing bowl, mix the flour, sugar, baking powder and chopped hazelnuts. In a smaller bowl, mix the milk, essences, lemon rind and oil. Combine the two mixtures and beat with a spoon.

Turn into the prepared cake tin. Bake for 40 minutes. Check if the centre of the cake is dry. If it is not, leave in the oven for another 5 minutes. Let the cake cool for about 10 minutes, then turn out and cool completely on a wire rack. Cut it into slices when cold.

Barm Brack

VEGAN

This is the famous Irish cake, ideal for rainy afternoons served with a cup of herb tea.

150 g (5 oz/¾ cup) caster sugar
300 ml (10 fl oz/1¼ cups) fennel seed or camomile tea
50 g (2 oz/¼ cup) butter or vegetable margarine
1 tablespoon chopped almonds (optional)
200 g (7 oz/1¼ cups) raisins
50 g (2 oz/¼ cup) glacé cherries, chopped
100 g (3½ oz/¾ cup) chopped mixed peel
300 g (10 oz/2½ cups) flour
5 teaspoons baking powder

❋ Melting method
❋ Cake tin: one 20 cm (8") round tin, greased and lined with greaseproof paper
❋ Oven temperature: 180°C (350°F/Gas Mark 4)
❋ Baking time: 60–70 minutes

In a mixing bowl, dissolve the sugar in the hot tea. Mix in the butter, almonds, raisins, cherries and mixed peel. When cold, sift the flour and the baking powder on top and mix well.

Turn into the prepared tin and bake for 1 hour. Check if the centre of the cake is dry. If it is not, leave in the oven for another 5 or 10 minutes. Let the cake cool for about 10 minutes, then turn out and cool completely on a wire rack. Remove the paper while the cake is still warm. Wrap cake in a fresh piece of paper and keep in an airtight tin.

Serve cut in wedges and, if you prefer, spread with butter.

Apple and Banana Cake

VEGAN

2 small apples, peeled and chopped
100 g (3½ oz/¾ cup) plain flour
1 teaspoon ground cinnamon
2 teaspoons baking powder
2 medium-sized bananas, mashed
50 ml (2 fl oz/¼ cup) yoghurt or soya yoghurt
2 tablespoons sunflower oil
50 g (2 oz/¼ cup) caster sugar

❀ One-step method
❀ Cake tin: one ½ kg (1 lb) loaf tin, greased and floured
❀ Oven temperature: 180°C (350°F/Gas Mark 4)
❀ Baking time: 30–35 minutes

Peel and chop the apples. Cook them over very low heat until soft. Leave to cool. In a mixing bowl, sift the flour, cinnamon and baking powder. Add the apples, mashed bananas, yoghurt, oil and sugar. Mix well with a spoon.

Spoon the mixture into the prepared tin and bake for 30 minutes. Check if the centre of the cake is dry. If it is not, leave in the oven for another 5 minutes. Let the cake cool for about 10 minutes, then turn out and cool completely on a wire rack.

❀ Variations: Instead of apples and bananas, use other fruit in season – pineapples, peaches, apricots, cherries, etc.

Apple Tea Bread

VEGAN

2 apples, peeled and chopped
200 g (7 oz/1½ cups) plain flour
1 teaspoon ground cinnamon
½ teaspoon ground cloves
50 g (2 oz/¼ cup) powdered milk or powdered soya milk
4 teaspoons baking powder
50 g (2 oz/¼ cup) raisins (optional)
100 g (3½ oz/½ cup) caster sugar
200 ml (7 fl oz/¾ cup) milk or soya milk

❈ One-step method
❈ Cake tin: one 1 kg (2 lb) loaf tin, greased and floured
❈ Oven temperature: 180°C (350°F/Gas Mark 4)
❈ Baking time: 30–35 minutes

Peel and chop the apples. Cook them over very low heat until soft. Allow to cool. In a mixing bowl, sift the flour, spices, powdered milk and baking powder. Add the apples, raisins and sugar. Mix well with a spoon, gradually adding the milk.

Spoon the mixture into the prepared loaf tin. Bake the cake for 30 minutes. Check if the centre of the cake is dry. If it is not, leave in the oven for another 5 minutes. Let the cake cool for about 10 minutes, then turn out and cool completely on a wire rack.

❈ Variations: Instead of apples, use pears, peaches, apricots or pineapple.

Lemon Tea Bread

VEGAN

150 ml (5 fl oz/⅔ cup) milk or soya milk
the juice and finely grated rind of 1 lemon
4 tablespoons butter or vegetable margarine
150 g (5 oz/¾ cup) caster sugar
200 g (7 oz/1½ cups) plain flour
½ teaspoon bicarbonate of soda
1 teaspoon baking powder

❀ Creaming method
❀ Cake tin: one 1 kg (2 lb) loaf tin, greased and floured
❀ Oven temperature: 180°C (350°F/Gas Mark 4)
❀ Baking time: 40–45 minutes

In a measuring jug or cup, mix the milk with the lemon juice. Leave for a few minutes until the milk curdles.

In a mixing bowl, beat the butter with the sugar until light and fluffy. Mix in the lemon rind. Add the flour mixed with bicarbonate of soda and baking powder, alternating with the curdled milk. Mix well and turn into the prepared loaf tin.

Bake for 40 minutes. Check if the centre of the cake is dry. If it is not, leave in the oven for another 5 minutes. Let the cake cool for about 10 minutes, then turn out and cool completely on a wire rack. Cut into slices when cold.

GÂTEAUX AND CHEESECAKES

Most cakes in this section are very rich. Some are decorated with fresh fruit. Choose fruits according to the season.

Granddad's Coconut Cake

1 quantity Quick Mix Sponge, coconut flavoured (see p. 54) made with 300 g flour,
   baked in a round cake tin, 25–30 cm (10"–12")

❋ Filling and icing:
50 g (2 oz/½ cup) toasted grated coconut
50 g (2 oz/½ cup) grated coconut for decoration
100 g (3½ oz/½ cup) unsalted butter or vegetable margarine
200 g (7 oz/1 cup) icing sugar
1 teaspoon vanilla essence
100 ml (3½ fl oz/½ cup) milk or soya milk
100 g (3½ oz/1 cup) grated coconut
Mock Chocolate leaves, cherries, fruit for decoration (optional)

Make the cake according to the recipe. When cold, cut into three layers. To toast the
grated coconut, place in a saucepan or frying pan over medium heat and stir for 3 to 4
minutes until golden brown. Allow to cool.

In a mixing bowl, cream the butter with the sugar. Add the vanilla and enough milk
to obtain a firm but soft cream. Beat for a few minutes longer.

Place one layer of cake on a serving plate. Spread ¼ of the filling and ½ cup grated
coconut. Repeat with the other two layers. Decorate the sides of the cake with the
golden, toasted coconut and the top with grated coconut. If you like, decorate with fruit
and/or Mock Chocolate leaves.

Cassata Cake

VEGAN

200 g (7 oz/1½ cups) plain flour
4 teaspoons baking powder
6 tablespoons sunflower oil
½ teaspoon vanilla essence
100 g (3½ oz/½ cup) caster sugar
200 ml (7 fl oz/¾ cup) milk or soya milk

❊ Filling:
250 g (½ lb/1¼ cups) fresh ricotta cheese or tofu
2 tablespoons cream or soya cream
5 tablespoons sugar
1 tablespoon orange juice
2 tablespoons chopped mixed peel
some extra chopped peel and glacé cherries for decoration

❊ One-step method
❊ Cake tin: one 20 × 30 cm (8" × 12") rectangular tin, greased and floured
❊ Oven temperature: 180°C (350°F/Gas Mark 4)
❊ Baking time: 20–25 minutes

In a mixing bowl, sift the flour and baking powder. Add the other ingredients. Beat for 1 minute with a spoon. Spoon the mixture into the tin. Bake for 20 to 25 minutes. Let the cake cool for 10 minutes and turn out. When cold, cut into four equal pieces widthways.

In the meantime, prepare the filling: break up the ricotta (or tofu), mix all ingredients together and beat for 2 or 3 minutes. Place one of the pieces of cake on a serving dish and spread with filling and chopped peel. Repeat with the other layers. Decorate with mixed peel and cherries. Serve cold.

Cheesecake 1

❋ Ingredients for the base:
100 g (3½ oz/¾ cup) plain flour
100 g (3½ oz/½ cup) caster sugar
100 g (3½ oz/½ cup) butter, softened
50 g (2 oz/¼ cup) ground walnuts (optional)

❋ Cake:
400 ml (14 fl oz/1⅔ cups) milk
4 teaspoons cornflour
150 g (5 oz/¾ cup) caster sugar
1 teaspoon vanilla essence
2 teaspoons agar-agar or other vegetable gelatine
400 g (14 oz/2 cups) fresh ricotta or curd cheese

❋ Topping:
150 ml (5 fl oz/⅔ cup) whipping cream, whipped
grapes, cherries, strawberries, peaches or oranges

❋ Cake tin: one 25 cm (10") round spring-clip tin, greased with butter
❋ Oven temperature: 180°C (350°F/Gas Mark 4)
❋ Baking time: 10–15 minutes

In a bowl, mix with your fingertips the flour, sugar and butter. Add the walnuts. Press the mixture evenly and firmly into the base of the tin. Bake for 10 to 15 minutes.

In the meantime, prepare the cake: In a saucepan, mix one cup of the milk with the cornflour. Heat until thick, stirring constantly. Add the sugar and the vanilla. Mix the agar-agar in the remaining milk and allow to thicken. If using a different vegetable gelatine, follow the manufacturer's instructions. In a mixing bowl, beat the cheese until creamy. Add the cornflour and agar-agar mixtures. Blend well. Pour on top of the pastry and refrigerate until set. Decorate with whipped cream and fruit. Serve cold.

Cheesecake 2

✿ Ingredients for the base:
100 g (3½ oz/¾ cup) flour
100 g (3½ oz/½ cup) caster sugar
100 g (3½ oz/½ cup) butter, softened

✿ Cake:
500 g (1¼ lb/2½ cups) fresh ricotta or curd cheese
100 ml (3½ fl oz/½ cup) fresh whipping or double cream
150 g (5 oz/¾ cup) caster sugar
2 tablespoons cornflour
1 tablespoon grated lemon rind

✿ Decoration:
Chantilly Cream
cherries, peaches, oranges, mandarins, strawberries or grapes

✿ Cake tin: one 25 cm (10") round spring-clip tin, greased with butter
✿ Oven temperature: 180°C (350°F/Gas Mark 4)
✿ Baking time: 1 hour

In a bowl, mix with your fingertips the flour, sugar and butter. Press the mixture evenly into the base of the tin. Bake for 10 to 15 minutes.

In the meantime, prepare the cake: In a mixing bowl, beat the cheese until creamy. Add the cream, sugar, cornflour and lemon rind.

Spoon the mixture onto the pastry and bake for 50 minutes. Cool and refrigerate for 3 hours. Decorate with Chantilly Cream and fruit. Serve cold.

Three-colour Cake

❁ Ingredients for the pink layer:
200 g (7 oz/1½ cups) self-raising flour
2 teaspoons baking powder
200 g (½ lb/1½ cups) strawberries
150 ml (5 fl oz/⅔ cup) yoghurt
4 tablespoons sunflower oil
100 g (3½ oz/½ cup) caster sugar

❁ Yellow and dark layers:
400 g (14 oz/3 cups) self-raising flour
4 teaspoons baking powder
200 ml (7 fl oz/¾ cup) yoghurt
200 g (7 oz/1 cup) caster sugar
200 ml (7 fl oz/¾ cup) milk
100 ml (3½ fl oz/½ cup) sunflower oil
1 teaspoon vanilla essence
50 g (2 oz/½ cups) carob powder, mixed with 2 tablespoons hot water

❁ Filling and icing:
1 quantity Chantilly Cream
200 g (½ lb/1½ cup) strawberries or other fruit in season

❁ Dry and wet method
❁ Cake tin: three 20 cm (8") round tins, greased and floured
❁ Oven temperature: 180°C (350°F/Gas Mark 4)
❁ Baking time: 20 minutes

The pink layer: Sift the flour and the baking powder. Mash the strawberries and mix them with the yoghurt and the oil. Mix this into the flour and add the sugar. Spoon the mixture into one of the prepared tins.

The yellow and dark layers: Sift the flour and the baking powder. In another bowl, mix the yoghurt, sugar, milk, oil and vanilla. Add the flour a bit at a time and mix well. Spoon half of the mixture into the second prepared tin. Add the dissolved carob powder to the remaining mixture and spoon it into the last cake tin.

Bake all three cakes for about 20 minutes. The vanilla layer will probably be cooked first. Allow the cakes to cool for 5 to 10 minutes and then turn out. Prepare the Chantilly Cream.

When cold, place the chocolate layer on a serving plate and cover it with one quarter of the Chantilly Cream. Follow with the other two layers, filling each. Spread the rest of the cream on top and around the cake. Decorate with strawberries or other fruit in season.

Delicacy Cake

1 quantity Shepherd's Cake (see p. 42) baked in a 20 × 30 cm (8" × 12") rectangular tin

✳ Sauce:
100 ml (3½ fl oz/½ cup) boiled milk
1 tablespoon carob powder
1 teaspoon vanilla essence
1 tablespoon sugar

✳ Filling and icing:
2 tablespoons butter
2 tablespoons carob powder
150 ml (5 fl oz/⅔ cup) milk
one 400 g tin (14 oz tin/approx. 1½ cups) condensed milk
1 teaspoon vanilla essence

Prepare the cake according to the recipe. When cold, cut it in half to form two layers. Place on a sheet of greaseproof paper.

Prepare the sauce: Boil the milk and pour 2 tablespoons of it into a cup. Dissolve the carob in the milk and pour back into the saucepan. Stir in the vanilla and sugar. Pierce the cake all over with a fork and spread the sauce on top. Let stand until all the sauce has been absorbed.

In the meantime, prepare the filling: In a saucepan, melt the butter and stir in the carob powder. Add the milk, the condensed milk and the vanilla. Stir constantly over low heat for about 20 minutes or until the mixture pulls away from the sides of the pan. Remove from the heat and allow to cool for 10 minutes.

Place half of the cake on a serving dish and spread with ⅓ of the filling. Place the other half of the cake on top and spread the rest of the icing over the top and sides. Allow to cool before serving.

Pineapple Cake

1 quantity Birthday Cake 1 (see p. 32) baked in a round tin

❄ Filling and icing:
25 g (1 oz/¼ cup) cornflour
150 g (5 oz/¾ cup) caster or granulated sugar
600 ml (1 pint/2½ cups) milk
200 g (7 oz/1 cup) unsalted butter
1 small pineapple, chopped and boiled in a little water with 2 tablespoons sugar, or 1
    tin of pineapple chunks
100 ml (3½ fl oz/½ cup) whipping or double cream
½ cup cherries for decoration

Make the cake according to the recipe. When cool, cut into three layers. Whip the cream until firm.

For the filling, mix the cornflour and the sugar with a little milk. Pour the rest of the milk into a saucepan and heat until boiling; then add the dissolved cornflour and sugar. Remove from the heat and cool. Add the butter a little at a time, mixing constantly.

Place one layer of cake on a serving plate. Spread with one third of the filling and some pineapple chunks. Repeat with the second and third layers of cake, finishing with a layer of filling.

Allow to cool and set. Decorate with piped whipped cream, a few pieces of pineapple and cherries. Refrigerate. Serve cold.

Black Forest Gâteau

1 quantity Birthday Cake 2 (see p. 34) baked in a round, 20–25 cm (8"–10") tin

❁ Filling and icing:
2 quantities Chantilly Cream (or 3 quantities for a very rich cream cake)
1 cup maraschino cherries (drained) for decoration
100 g (3½ oz/½ cup) carob pieces or Mock Chocolate

Make the cake according to the recipe. When cold, cut it into three layers. Divide the Chantilly Cream into two parts.

Chop ¾ cup of cherries and add them to half the cream. This will be the filling. Place one layer of cake on a serving dish. Spread half of the amount of filling on top. Add the second layer of cake and fill.

Spread the other half of Chantilly Cream on the top and sides of the cake.

Decorate with whole cherries and grated carob pieces. If you wish, reserve some of the cream and pipe swirls on top of the cake. Serve cold.

Gauranga Cake

VEGAN

200 ml (7 fl oz/¾ cup) milk or soya milk
100 ml (3½ fl oz/½ cup) yoghurt or soya yoghurt
100 ml (3½ fl oz/½ cup) sunflower oil
200 g (7 oz/1 cup) caster sugar
the juice and grated rind of 1 large orange
300 g (10 oz/2½ cups) self-raising flour
3 teaspoons baking powder

❈ Filling and icing:
the juice of 1 large orange
1 quantity Butter Icing (orange flavour)
2 small tangerines (peeled and divided into segments) or 1 small tin mandarins or
    oranges (drained) for decoration

❈ One-step method
❈ Cake tin: one 20 × 30 cm (8" × 12") tin, greased and floured
❈ Oven temperature: 180°C (350°F/Gas Mark 4)
❈ Baking time: 20–25 minutes

In a bowl, mix the milk, yoghurt, oil, sugar, juice and orange rind. Sift the flour and
baking powder on top. Beat for 1 minute with a spoon, and turn into the prepared cake
tin. Bake for 20 to 25 minutes. Allow the cake to cool for 10 minutes and then turn out
onto a sheet of greaseproof paper. Prick the cake with a fork and pour the orange juice
on top.

When cold, cut into two layers. Place one layer on a serving dish and spread ⅓ of the
filling on top. Cover with the other half of the cake and spread the rest of the icing on
the top and sides of the cake. Decorate with mandarins or oranges.

Nrisimha Cake

VEGAN

50 g (2 oz/¼ cup) butter or vegetable margarine
150 g (5 oz/¾ cup) caster sugar
75 ml (2½ fl oz/⅓ cup) sunflower oil
100 ml (3½ fl oz/½ cup) yoghurt or soya yoghurt
60 ml (2 fl oz/¼ cup) honey or golden syrup
200 ml (7 fl oz/¾ cup) milk or soya milk
300 g (10 oz/2½ cups) self-raising flour
50 g (2 oz/½ cup) cornflour
3 teaspoons baking powder
2 teaspoons mixed spice

❀ Filling: 1 quantity Fruit and Nut Filling
❀ Icing: 1 quantity Butter Icing
chopped mixed peel for decoration

❀ Creaming method
❀ Cake tin: one 20 × 30 cm (8" × 12") rectangular tin, greased and floured
❀ Oven temperature: 180°C (350°F/Gas Mark 4)
❀ Baking time: 25–30 minutes

In a mixing bowl, cream the butter and the sugar until light and fluffy. Add the oil, yoghurt, honey and milk. Sift the flour, cornflour, baking powder and spice on top. Beat for 2 minutes with a spoon. Turn into the tin and bake for 25 minutes or until dry and golden.

When cold, cut into two layers. Place one layer on a serving dish and spread with Fruit and Nut Filling. Top with the other half of the cake and spread the Butter Icing on the top and sides of the cake. Decorate with chopped peel.

Fruit Gâteau

1 quantity Quick Mix Sponge (see p. 54) made with 300 g flour, baked in a round tin, 20 or 25 cm (8" or 10")

✿ Filling and icing:

1 quantity Crème Pâtisserie

3 cups chopped fruit: pineapple, mango, peaches, strawberries, kiwi, apricots, etc.
   Reserve the best pieces for decoration

50 g (2 oz/½ cup) split almonds for decoration

250 ml (8 fl oz/1 cup) vegetarian orange-flavoured jelly (optional)

Make the cake according to the recipe. When cold, cut into three layers. Make the Crème Pâtisserie and allow to cool. Place one layer of cake on a serving dish. Spread with ⅓ of the filling and ⅓ of the fruit. Repeat with the second layer, then top with the last layer of cake.

Spread the rest of the filling on the top and sides of the cake. Decorate the sides with split almonds and the top with pieces of fruit. If you wish, glaze with orange-flavoured jelly. Refrigerate. Serve cold.

Almond Cream Cake

Vegan

1 quantity Quick Mix Sponge (see p. 54) made with 200 g flour, baked in a 25 cm (10") ring mould

❀ Filling and icing:
50 g (2 oz/¼ cup) chopped almonds
100 g (3½ oz/½ cup) unsalted butter or vegetable margarine
200 g (7 oz/1 cup) icing sugar
½ teaspoon almond essence
100 ml (3½ fl oz/½ cup) milk or soya milk
a few maraschino cherries for decoration

Make the cake according to the recipe. When cold, cut into three layers. Toast the chopped almonds in a saucepan over medium heat for a few minutes until golden brown.

In a mixing bowl, cream the butter with the sugar. Add the essence and enough milk to obtain a firm but soft cream. Beat for a few minutes longer.

Place one layer of cake on a serving plate. Spread with ¼ of the filling and ⅓ of the chopped almonds. Repeat with the second layer and then top with the last layer of cake. Spread the remaining icing on the top and sides of the cake. Decorate with the rest of the almonds and a few cherries.

❀ Variations: Use walnuts, pecans, hazelnuts or cashew nuts instead of almonds. Use vanilla instead of almond essence.

Mango Gâteau

1 quantity Birthday Cake 1 (see p. 32) baked in a 25 cm (10") round tin

❁ Filling and icing:
600 ml (1 pint/2½ cups) Chantilly Cream
2 mangoes
2 tablespoons lemon juice
½ cup grated coconut

Make the cake according to the recipe. When cold, cut into three layers. Prepare the Chantilly Cream. Peel the mangoes and cut them into thin slices. Dip them into lemon juice. Reserve the best slices for decoration.

Place one layer of cake on a serving dish. Spread with ¼ of the cream. Add some mango and grated coconut. Add the second layer and fill. Top with the third layer. Spread the rest of the cream on top and on the sides of the cake and decorate with the best slices of mango.

Refrigerate for 2 to 3 hours before serving.

Swiss Roll

VEGAN

200 ml (7 fl oz/¾ cup) milk or soya milk
a few drops lemon juice
4 tablespoons butter or vegetable margarine
50 g (2 oz/¼ cup) sugar
1 tablespoon honey or molasses
100 g (3½ oz/¾ cup) flour
75 g (3 oz/⅔ cup) cornflour
1 teaspoon baking powder
1 tablespoon icing sugar for dredging (optional)

❋ Filling and icing: 4 tablespoons jam or ½ quantity Fruit and Nut Filling or ½ quantity Butter Icing

❋ Creaming method
❋ Cake tin: 1 Swiss roll tin or a 20 × 30 cm (8" × 12") rectangular tin, greased and floured
❋ Oven temperature: 180°C (350°F/Gas Mark 4)
❋ Baking time: 10–15 minutes

In a cup, mix the milk with the lemon juice. In a mixing bowl, cream the butter and the sugar until light and fluffy. Add the honey or molasses and the milk and beat. Sift the flour, cornflour and baking powder on top. Combine all the ingredients together. Pour into the prepared cake tin and bake for 10 to 15 minutes.

Allow to cool for no more than 5 minutes, then turn out onto a slightly damp tea towel. Tucking in the edge of the towel, gently roll the cake up in the towel and leave for a few moments. Carefully unroll the cake and spread it with the filling. Then roll the cake again (this time without the towel). Leave to cool.

Dredge with icing sugar. Alternatively, for special occasions, decorate with ½ quantity Chocolate Butter Icing, glacé cherries and Mock Chocolate leaves.

Neapolitan Cake

VEGAN

300 g (10 oz/2½ cups) flour
4 teaspoons baking powder
200 g (7 oz/1 cup) caster sugar
150 g (5 oz/¾ cup) butter
2 tablespoons milk or soya milk
50 ml (2 fl oz/¼ cup) yoghurt or vegan yoghurt
the rind of 1 lemon, finely grated
100 g (3½ oz/½ cup) chopped almonds

✿ Filling :
1 quantity Chantilly Cream or Vegan Chantilly Cream

✿ Icing:
1 quantity Glacé Icing
½ cup maraschino cherries, drained

✿ Rub-in method
✿ Cake tins: two or more 20–25 cm (8"–10") round tins, greased and floured
✿ Oven temperature: 180°C (350°F/Gas Mark 4)
✿ Baking time: 10 minutes for each layer

In a mixing bowl, sift the flour, baking powder and sugar, and mix well. Rub in the butter. Add the milk, yoghurt, lemon rind and almonds, and continue mixing to form a soft and pliable pastry. Divide into 5 parts and roll into 5 balls. Roll out each ball to 20 cm (8"). Sprinkle them with flour and bake each one for 10 minutes. Allow to cool. Place one layer on a serving dish and spread with ¼ of the Chantilly Cream. Continue adding cake layers and filling them, finishing with a layer of cake. Spread the Glacé Icing on top and decorate with cherries.

Strawberry Gâteau

1 quantity Birthday Cake 1 (see p. 32)

❀ Filling and icing:
150 ml (5 fl oz/⅔ cup) whipping cream
100 g (3½ oz/½ cup) unsalted butter
200 g (7 oz/1 cup) icing sugar
250 g (½ lb/1½ cups) chopped strawberries
125 g (¼ lb/¾ cup) sliced strawberries for decoration
1 kiwi fruit, sliced toasted cashew nuts and chopped peel for decoration (optional)

Make the cake according to the recipe. When cold, cut into three layers. Whip the cream till light and fluffy.

In a mixing bowl, cream the butter and the sugar. Fold in the whipped cream. Divide the mixture into two parts. Add the chopped strawberries to one of them. Use this for the filling and the other mixture for the icing.

Place one layer of cake on a serving dish. Spread with half of the quantity of filling and add and fill the second layer. Top with the third layer of cake.

Spread the icing on the top and sides of the cake and decorate with sliced strawberries, kiwi, cashew nuts and chopped peel. Serve cold.

Grandmother's Fridge Cake

1 quantity Coconut Biscuits (see below)
one 400 g tin (14 oz tin/approx. 1½ cups) condensed milk
200 ml (7 fl oz/¾ cup) cold milk
1 tablespoon sugar
a little butter for greasing
50 g (2 oz/¼ cup) chopped walnuts

Place the tin of condensed milk in a deep saucepan and cover it with water. Boil for 2 hours, checking the water level regularly. Alternatively, cook in a pressure cooker; the cooking time is then reduced to 1 hour. Allow to cool completely before opening the tin – do not attempt to open the tin while it is hot.

In a mixing bowl, mix the milk with the sugar. Moisten the biscuits in the mixture.

Grease a deep dish with butter and line it with a layer of biscuits. Cover with a layer of condensed milk. Repeat until all ingredients have been used. Decorate with walnuts. Refrigerate for 3 hours before serving.

Coconut Biscuits

100 g (3½ oz/½ cup) butter or vegetable margarine
200 g (7 oz/1½ cups) flour
100 g (3½ oz/½ cup) sugar
50 g (2 oz/½ cup) grated coconut
2 tablespoons milk

With your fingertips, rub the butter into the flour. Add the sugar, coconut and milk. Mix until the mixture is smooth and firm. Roll out onto a floured surface to 3 mm (⅛") thick. Cut into small rectangles and place them onto a greased baking tin. Bake at 180°C (350°F/Gas Mark 4) for 15 minutes. Allow to cool in the cake tin.

German Apple Cake

VEGAN

This is similar to an English apple pie, but with a lighter pastry.

❁ Ingredients for the pastry:
300 g (10 oz/2½ cups) plain flour
150 g (5 oz/¾ cup) butter or vegetable margarine
150 g (5 oz/¾ cup) caster sugar
2 tablespoons crème fraîche or double cream or soya cream

❁ Filling:
50 g (2 oz/¼ cup each) almonds and hazelnuts, chopped
1 kg (2 lb) cooking apples
150 g (5 oz/¾ cup) sugar
1 teaspoon cinnamon
100 ml (3½ fl oz/½ cup) water
50 g (2 oz/¼ cup) raisins
1 tablespoon icing sugar to dredge

❁ Rub-in method
❁ Cake tin: one 25 cm (10") round loose-bottomed or spring-clip tin, greased and floured
❁ Oven temperature: 180°C (350°F/Gas Mark 4)
❁ Baking time: 40 minutes

Sift the flour into a bowl. Rub in the butter well. Add the sugar and cream and mix to form a stiff paste. Divide the pastry roughly into three parts. Roll out one third and use it to cover the base of the prepared tin. The pastry is rather sticky, so roll it out between two sheets of greaseproof paper.

Sprinkle half of the nuts on top. Bake for 10 minutes in the centre of the oven. Leave the pastry to cool for 10 to 15 minutes.

In the meantime, prepare the filling: Peel, core and chop the apples. Mix them with the sugar, cinnamon and water. Cook until soft. Roll out another third of the pastry into a long strip to line the sides of the tin. Where it meets the base, pinch edges of pastry well together to seal. Fill with the apple mixture and sprinkle the raisins and the rest of the nuts on top. Cover with the last third of pastry. Press with a fork to seal. Return the cake to the oven and bake for another 30 minutes. When cool, dredge with icing sugar.

Fridge Cake

1 quantity Quick Mix Sponge (see p. 54) made with 200 g flour, baked in an 18 × 25 cm
    (7" × 10") rectangular tin
1 quantity Crème Pâtisserie (vanilla or chocolate flavour)
200 ml (7 fl oz/¾ cup) boiled milk
1 tablespoon sugar
1 teaspoon vanilla essence
200 ml (7 fl oz/¾ cup) fresh whipping or double cream

Prepare the sponge as in the recipe. Bake until firm and dry, then switch off the oven. Remove the cake from the oven, cut into squares and return to the oven. Leave it there until cool and hard. In the meantime, prepare the Crème Pâtisserie.

Mix the milk with the sugar and vanilla. Dip each cake square in this mixture and place it in a deep serving dish. Cover with a layer of Crème Pâtisserie. Repeat until all the ingredients have been used.

Spread whipped cream on top and refrigerate for at least 3 hours before serving. This cake may be frozen, but remember to remove from the freezer about half an hour before serving.

Tiramisù

VEGAN

This is a moist, delicious Italian dessert, ideal for dinner parties.

1 quantity Quick Mix Sponge (see p. 54) made with 200 g flour, baked in an 18 × 25 cm
(7" × 10") rectangular tin
200 ml (7 fl oz/¾ cup) strong barley coffee
½ teaspoon artificial brandy flavour (optional)
300 ml (10 fl oz/1¼ cups) milk or any plant milk
2 tablespoons cornflour
75 g (2½ oz/3 tablespoons) sugar
250 g (½ lb/1¼ cups) mascarpone cheese or soft silken tofu
½ teaspoon vanilla essence
1 tablespoon carob powder

Prepare the sponge according to the recipe. Bake until firm and dry and switch off the oven. Remove the cake from the oven, cut into squares and return to the oven. Leave it there until cool and hard. The pieces of cake should feel almost as hard as cookies.

Prepare the coffee and, when cold, pour into a deep dish and mix in the brandy flavour. Place the pieces of cake into the coffee and leave them for 10 minutes, until all the liquid has been absorbed.

In a saucepan, mix the milk and the cornflour. Cook over low heat until thick. Stir in the sugar. Add the mascarpone cheese and let the mixture boil, stirring constantly. Remove from the heat and stir in the vanilla.

Pour half of the mixture into a deep heat-proof dish. Arrange the pieces of cake on top and then pour on the other half of the mixture. Smooth the surface with the back of a spoon. Allow to cool for 10 minutes. Sprinkle with carob powder by sieving it through a dry tea strainer. Refrigerate for 1 to 3 hours before serving.

Mille Sfoglie

Vegan

1 quantity Easy Puff Pastry (see p. 174) or 500 g (1 lb) frozen puff pastry
1 quantity Chantilly Cream or Vegan Chantilly Cream
1 quantity Crème Pâtisserie
2 spoonfuls apricot jam (optional)
100 g (3½ oz/½ cup) pistachio nuts
lime slivers, chopped mixed peel, strawberries or cherries for decoration

Cut the puff pastry into four parts. Roll out each one into 25-cm (10") circles. Place circles onto greased plates or cake tins and bake them in a hot oven (190°C/375°F/Gas Mark 5) for 10 minutes. Remove from oven and allow to cool. Prepare the Chantilly Cream and Crème Pâtisserie. When the layers of puff pastry are cold, place one onto a serving plate and cover with one third of the Crème Pâtisserie. Cover with the other circles of pastry and fill, ending with pastry. If using jam, spread it between one of the layers of pastry and Crème Pâtisserie.

Spread half of the Chantilly Cream on the sides of the cake. Spread the chopped nuts onto a sheet of greaseproof paper. Very carefully roll the cake on top of the nuts until uniformly coated. Spread the rest of the cream on the top of the cake and decorate with strawberries or cherries, pistachios, lime slivers and peel.

Easy Puff Pastry

250 g (8 oz/2 cups) flour
a pinch of salt
150 g (5 oz/¾ cup) cold butter or vegetable margarine
100 ml (3½ fl oz/½ cup) ice-cold water
1 teaspoon lemon juice

In a mixing bowl, sift the flour and salt. Using a round-topped knife, cut the butter into 5 mm (¼") cubes and cut them into the flour. Stir in the water and lemon juice and gather together with your fingertips.

Shape into a block and place on a floured surface. Roll out into a rectangle measuring about 30 × 15 cm (12" × 6"). Fold the rectangle into three, turn it round (but not over) and roll out again. Repeat once more.

Wrap in a tea towel and refrigerate for 30 minutes before using it in the recipe.

Sachertorte

Vegan

This is obviously not the same recipe as found in the Hotel Sacher in Vienna, as that one is a highly valued secret.

100 g (3½ oz/½ cup) carob drops or carob pieces or Mock Chocolate
2 tablespoons sunflower oil
100 ml (3½ fl oz/½ cup) yoghurt or soya yoghurt
75 g (3 oz/½ cup) caster sugar
50 g (2 oz/¼ cup) ground almonds
100 g (3½ oz/¾ cup) plain flour
2 teaspoons baking powder
1–2 tablespoons warmed apricot jam

❀ Icing:
50 g (2 oz/¼ cup) carob pieces or carob drops
1 tablespoon unsalted butter or vegetable margarine
100 g (3½ oz/½ cup) icing sugar, sifted
1½ tablespoons warm water

❀ Creaming method
❀ Cake tin: one 20 cm (8") round tin, greased and lined with a round of greaseproof
   paper
❀ Oven temperature: 180°C (350°F/Gas Mark 4)
❀ Baking time: 30 minutes

Put the carob pieces into a basin standing over a saucepan of hot water. Leave until melted, stirring occasionally. Into the melted carob beat the oil, yoghurt, sugar, almonds, flour and baking powder.

Spoon the mixture into the prepared tin. Bake for 30 minutes or until the centre of the cake is dry. Remove from the oven and allow to cool for 10 minutes. Turn out onto a wire rack. When lukewarm, turn the cake right way up and brush with apricot jam.

For the icing, put the carob pieces in a basin standing over a saucepan of hot water. Add the butter and stir. Mix in the icing sugar and water. Stir thoroughly. Spread the icing over the top and sides of the cake. Some icing will drip through the wire rack, so put a plate underneath. Leave undisturbed until the icing has set. Cut into portions and serve plain or with whipped cream.

Apfelstrudel

VEGAN

250 g (8 oz/2 cups) plain flour
a pinch of salt
2 tablespoons crème fraîche or vegan cream
100 ml (3½ fl oz/½ cup) water
150 g (5 oz/¾ cup) butter, melted
200 g (7 oz/1 cup) chopped hazelnuts
1 kg (2 lb) apples
a few drops lemon juice
100 g (3½ oz/¾ cup) raisins
50 g (2 oz/¼ cup) ground almonds
125 g (4 oz/½ cup) sugar
1 teaspoon cinnamon
1 tablespoon icing sugar

❈ Oven temperature: 200°C (400°F/Gas Mark 6)
❈ Cake tin: one large rectangular tray or baking sheet, greased
❈ Baking time: 1 hour

Mix together the flour, salt, water, cream and ⅔ of the melted butter. Knead into a very soft dough. Wrap in cling film, cover with a bowl and leave to rest in a warm place for 30 minutes.

In the meantime, roast the hazelnuts until golden brown, let them cool and grate or finely chop them. Peel the apples and cut them into thin slices. Toss them with lemon juice.

Cover a table or work surface with a patterned tea towel and dust it with flour. Place the dough in the middle and start stretching it to the size of the towel without allowing the dough to tear.

Grease your hands and the dough from time to time with the rest of the butter. The dough should be very thin – almost transparent – so that the towel's pattern begins to show through the pastry.

Sprinkle the chopped hazelnuts on top, then the apples, raisins, almonds, sugar and cinnamon.

With the help of the cloth, roll up the strudel. If the dough sticks to the towel, gently prize it off with a knife dusted with flour. Tip the strudel carefully onto the prepared tray and brush the top and sides with the leftover butter. Bake for 1 hour in the bottom part of the oven.

When the strudel is golden brown, smear it once more with butter. Remove from the oven and sift icing sugar on top. Serve warm or cold, cut up into slices.

Swedish Sockerkaka

This traditional Scandinavian cake is baked in a fluted ring tin, but an ordinary ring tin or even a regular cake tin can be used instead.

150 g (5 oz/¾ cup) butter
200 ml (7 fl oz/¾ cup) milk
200 ml (7 fl oz/¾ cup) yoghurt
200 g (7 oz/1 cup) caster sugar
the rind of 1 lemon, finely grated, or ½ teaspoon vanilla essence
    or 4 teaspoons vanilla sugar
300 g (10 oz/2½ cups) flour
4 teaspoons baking powder
1 tablespoon icing sugar

❀ Melting method
❀ Cake tin: one 25 × 9 cm (12 cup) fluted ring tin, greased and floured
❀ Oven temperature: 170°C (330°F/Gas Mark 3)
❀ Baking time: 40–50 minutes

Melt the butter. Mix in the milk, yoghurt, sugar and lemon rind or vanilla essence. Sift together the flour, baking powder and vanilla sugar, if using any. Combine the dry and wet ingredients together.

Turn into the prepared cake tin and bake for 40 minutes. Check if the cake is ready. If it is not, leave for another 10 minutes. Remove from the oven and cool for 20 minutes. Turn out onto a wire cooling rack. Dredge with icing sugar. Alternatively, cover with Lemon Icing. Let stand for a few hours or overnight before cutting into wedges.

Fruit Sockerkaka

1 quantity Swedish Sockerkaka (see p. 178)
150 g (5 oz/1 cup) chopped nuts, glacé cherries and dried fruit

Follow the recipe for Swedish Sockerkaka, but mix the fruit and nuts into the flour. Increase the baking time to 50 to 60 minutes.

Tiger Cake

1 quantity Swedish Sockerkaka (see p. 178)
50 g (2 oz/½ cup) carob powder

Prepare the mixture as for Swedish Sockerkaka. Divide it into two bowls and sift the carob into one of them. Mix well.

Spoon or pour half of the carob mixture into the prepared tin, cover it with the light-coloured mixture and then with the remaining carob mixture. Carefully swirl the mixture with a knife or a spoon handle.

Bake for 50 to 60 minutes in the lower part of the oven. Remove from the oven and cool for 20 minutes. Turn out onto a wire cooling rack. Let stand for a few hours or overnight before cutting into wedges.

Upside Down Cake

1 tablespoon butter
1 tablespoon sugar
4 pineapple rings or peach halves
5 cherries, stoned
200 g (7 oz/1½ cups) plain flour
2 teaspoons baking powder
½ teaspoon bicarbonate of soda
½ teaspoon vanilla essence
50 ml (2 fl oz/¼ cup) water
150 ml (5 fl oz/⅔ cup) milk
100 ml (3½ fl oz/½ cup) condensed milk
2 tablespoons sunflower oil
½ quantity Chantilly Cream

❀ One-step method
❀ Cake tin: two 20 cm (8") round tins (see recipe)
❀ Oven temperature: 180°C (350°F/Gas Mark 4)
❀ Baking time: 20 minutes

First prepare the cake tins: grease one of them with butter and sprinkle with flour. In the other, melt 1 tablespoon butter and sprinkle with 1 tablespoon sugar, then arrange the pineapple rings or peach halves, placing a cherry in the middle of each and one in the centre of the tin.

In a mixing bowl, sift together the flour, the baking powder and the bicarbonate of soda. Mix in the other ingredients. Divide the mixture into the two tins and bake for 20 minutes. Allow to cool for 15 minutes and turn out. When cold, place the plain half on a serving dish and spread with Chantilly Cream. Place the other half on top. Serve cold.

Ekadashi Coconut Cake

150 g (5 oz/1¼ cups) milk powder
150 g (5 oz/1¼ cups) potato flour
200 g (7 oz/1 cup) caster sugar
1 teaspoon bicarbonate of soda
50 g (2 oz/¼ cup) butter
50 g (2 oz/½ cup) grated coconut
2 mashed bananas
100 ml (3½ fl oz/½ cup) yoghurt
the finely grated rinds of 1 lemon and 1 orange
100 g (3½ oz/½ cup) chopped, roasted hazelnuts

❁ Dry and wet method
❁ Cake tin: one 25 cm (10") round tin, greased
❁ Oven temperature: 170°C (330°F/Gas Mark 3)
❁ Baking time: 20–30 minutes

Sift together the milk powder, potato flour, sugar and bicarbonate. Melt the butter and toast the coconut in it until golden brown.

In another bowl, mash the bananas, and mix in the yoghurt, rinds and toasted coconut. Add the dry ingredients and nuts and beat with a spoon.

Spoon the mixture into the prepared tin and bake for about 20 to 30 minutes. Test with a skewer or toothpick; the middle of the cake should be dry. Remove from the oven and cool for 10 minutes. Turn out onto a wire cooling rack.

When cold, cut the cake in half horizontally and fill and decorate with whipped cream and chopped fresh fruit.

Apple Pudding Cake

150 g (5 oz/¾ cup) butter
300 g (10 oz/2½ cups) plain flour
150 g (5 oz/¾ cup) caster sugar
2 tablespoons crème fraîche or double cream

❀ Filling:
1 kg (2 lb) cooking apples
150 g (5 oz/¾ cup) sugar
1 teaspoon cinnamon
1 teaspoon ground cardamom
a pinch of ground cloves
the rinds of 1 lemon and 1 orange, finely grated
1 teaspoon vanilla sugar or ½ teaspoon vanilla essence
100 g (3½ oz/1 cup) cornflour

❀ Icing:
1 quantity Chantilly Cream, mixed with a few drops bitter almond essence
50 g (2 oz/¼ cup) chopped almonds

❀ Rub-in method
❀ Cake tin: one 25 cm (10") round loose-bottomed or spring-clip tin, greased and
  floured
❀ Oven temperature: 180°C (350°F/Gas Mark 4)
❀ Baking time: 10 minutes plus 15–20 minutes

Prepare the pastry: rub the butter into the flour with your fingertips until the mixture
looks like fine breadcrumbs. Add the sugar and cream and draw the mixture together.
Press just over half the pastry into the bottom of the prepared tin. Bake for 10 minutes.
Set aside to cool.

Peel, core and chop the apples. Cook them over low heat until soft. Mash them and allow to cool. Mix in sugar, spices, rind, vanilla and cornflour. Heat the mixture, stirring continuously, until it thickens. Remove from the heat.

Line the sides of the cooled tin with the rest of the pastry. Spoon the apple mixture into the tin and bake for another 15–20 minutes. When cold, spread with the Chantilly Cream. Sprinkle the almonds on top.

Raspberry Gâteau

Vegan

1 quantity Birthday Cake 1 (see p. 32) baked in a round 20 cm (8") tin

❋ Filling and icing:
2 quantities Chantilly Cream or Vegan Chantilly Cream
2 cups raspberries
100 g (3½ oz/1 cup) dried apples or shredded coconut
a few cashew nuts and hazelnuts for decoration

Make the cake according to the recipe. When cold, cut it into four layers. Divide the Chantilly Cream into two parts.

Add the raspberries to one of the parts. This will be the filling. Place one layer of cake on a serving dish. Spread half of the amount of filling on top. Layer the cake and filling, ending with the cake.

Spread the other half of Chantilly Cream on the top and sides of the assembled cake. Decorate with dried apples or coconut and nuts. Serve cold.

PUDDINGS

*I*n this section there are recipes for two kinds of cakes: very moist cakes which resemble puddings and should be treated as such – heavy, syrupy, sugary treats; and steamed puddings traditionally cooked in a pudding basin.

These puddings can be steamed either in a saucepan over low heat or in an oven, which is an economical alternative if you are making several. If you are steaming the puddings in an oven, pour the mixture into metal or glass basins and place them on a baking tray half-filled with hot water. Cook for as long as indicated in the recipe.

Alternatively, pour the mixture into a metal or Pyrex bowl or basin and place it in a saucepan half-filled with hot water. Cover the saucepan and let the pudding steam over low heat.

In either case, remember to top up with hot water as the level lowers.

Crazy Carob Pudding

VEGAN

200 g (7 oz/1 cup) butter or vegetable margarine
25 g (1 oz/¼ cup) carob powder
200 g (7 oz/1½ cups) plain flour
200 g (7 oz/1 cup) caster sugar
4 teaspoons baking powder
1 teaspoon salt
200 ml (7 fl oz/¾ cup) milk or soya milk
½ teaspoon vanilla essence

❋ Syrup:
200 g (7 oz/1 cup) any unrefined sugar
100 g (3½ oz/1 cup) carob powder
400 ml (14 fl oz/1⅔ cups) boiling water

❋ Melting method
❋ Cake tin: one 20 cm (8") ring mould, greased and floured
❋ Oven temperature: 190°C (375°F/Gas Mark 5)
❋ Baking time: 25 minutes

Melt the butter and dissolve the carob powder in it.

In a mixing bowl, mix the flour, sugar, baking powder and salt. Add the milk and vanilla. Stir in the butter-carob mixture.

Spoon the mixture into the prepared cake tin. Add the syrup: Sprinkle with the sugar and carob powder and then pour the boiling water on top. Bake for 25 minutes. Cool for 30 minutes, and turn out into a deep dish.

Sponge Pudding

VEGAN

200 g (7 oz/1½ cups) self-raising flour
2 teaspoons baking powder
the rind of 1 lemon, finely grated
100 g (3½ oz/½ cup) caster sugar
½ teaspoon cinnamon
100 g (3½ oz/½ cup) vegetable margarine
100 ml (3½ fl oz/½ cup) apple juice
4 tablespoons honey or golden syrup

❀ Rub-in method
❀ Cake tin: one 1-litre (2-pint) pudding basin, greased
❀ Oven temperature: 160°C (325°F/Gas Mark 3); alternatively, it can be steamed in a saucepan
❀ Steaming time: 2 hours

Mix together the flour, baking powder, lemon rind, sugar and cinnamon. Rub in the margarine. Add the juice and stir. Spoon into the pudding basin and cover with foil. Steam for 2 hours. Pour the honey on top just before serving.

❀ Variations:
1. Add 1 grated medium cooking apple.
2. Add ½ cup raisins, sultanas or currants.

Apple Ring

VEGAN

200 g (7 oz/1½ cups) plain flour
½ teaspoon salt
½ teaspoon ground ginger
2 teaspoons baking powder
½ teaspoon bicarbonate of soda
100 g (3½ oz/½ cup) light brown soft sugar
75 g (3 oz/⅓ cup) vegetable margarine
25 g (1 oz/2 tablespoons) treacle
100 g (3½ oz/½ cup) golden syrup
150 ml (5 fl oz/⅔ cup) milk or soya milk

✻ Filling:
2 large cooking apples
the juice of 1 lemon
½ tablespoon grated lemon rind
100 ml (3½ fl oz/½ cup) water
2 tablespoons sugar
2 teaspoons arrowroot

✻ Dry and wet method
✻ Cake tin: one 20 cm (8") ring mould, greased and floured
✻ Oven temperature: 180°C (350°F/Gas Mark 4)
✻ Baking time: 35 minutes

Sift the flour, salt, ginger, baking powder and bicarbonate of soda into a large bowl. Place the rest of the ingredients except the milk in a saucepan and heat gently, until liquid. Remove from the heat and add the milk. Pour this into the dry mixture and beat with a spoon.

Pour the mixture into the prepared tin and bake for 35 minutes. Leave to cool for 5 minutes and turn out onto a serving plate.

In the meantime, prepare the filling. Peel and slice the apples and boil them in the lemon juice over low heat for 5 minutes. Add the lemon rind and mix gently. Remove from the heat and spoon into the centre of the ring.

Pour the water and sugar into the saucepan and mix in the arrowroot. Boil over low heat. Gently brush the ring with the mixture and pour the rest over the apples.

Sweetcorn Pudding

200 g (7 oz/1 cup) sweetcorn, boiled
200 g (7 oz/1½ cups) plain flour
4 teaspoons baking powder
100 ml (3½ fl oz/½ cup) milk
4 tablespoons sunflower oil
one 400 g tin (14 oz tin/approx. 1½ cups) condensed milk

❀ One-step method
❀ Cake tin: one 20 cm (8") ring mould, greased and floured
❀ Oven temperature: 180°C (350°F/Gas Mark 4)
❀ Baking time: 25 minutes

In a mixing bowl, combine all ingredients except the condensed milk. Turn into the prepared cake tin and bake for 25 minutes.

Leave to cool for about 10 minutes and turn out into a deep dish. While the cake is still warm, prick its surface with a fork and pour the condensed milk over it. Refrigerate and serve when all the condensed milk has been absorbed.

Christmas Pudding 1

VEGAN

50 g (2 oz/⅓ cup) wholemeal flour
½ teaspoon baking powder
¼ teaspoon ground nutmeg
½ teaspoon mixed spice
200 g (7 oz/2 cups) breadcrumbs
100 g (3½ oz/½ cup) vegetable suet or grated vegetable fat
200 g (7 oz/1¼ cups) raisins
200 g (7 oz/1¼ cups) sultanas
200 g (7 oz/1¼ cups) currants
100 g (3½ oz/¾ cup) mixed peel
50 g (2 oz/¼ cup) chopped almonds
250 ml (8 fl oz/1 cup) orange juice
100 g (3½ oz/½ cup) muscovado sugar

❋ Dry and wet method
❋ Cake tins: two 1 litre (2 pint) pudding basins, greased
❋ Oven temperature: 160°C (325°F/Gas Mark 3); alternatively, steam the pudding in a saucepan
❋ Steaming time: 2 hours

Sift the flour, baking powder, nutmeg and spice. Mix in the breadcrumbs, suet, fruit, peel and almonds. In a measuring jug, combine the juice and sugar.

Combine the wet and dry mixtures, beat well for one minute. Divide into the prepared pudding basins. Cover the basins with greaseproof paper. Steam them in the oven or in a saucepan for approximately 2 hours. Store the puddings in the refrigerator. Before serving, steam them for about one hour.

Christmas Pudding 2

VEGAN

150 g (5 oz/1¼ cups) plain flour
1½ teaspoons baking powder
2 teaspoons mixed spice
300 g (10 oz/3 cups) fresh breadcrumbs
200 g (7 oz/1 cup) shredded vegetable suet
1 kg (2¼ lb/8 cups) mixed dried fruit, including peel
50 g (2 oz/¼ cup) chopped walnuts
300 ml (10 fl oz/1¼ cups) apple juice
the juice and grated rind of 1 lemon
200 g (7 oz/1 cup) muscovado sugar

❀ Dry and wet method
❀ Cake tins: two 1 litre (2 pint) or four ½ litre (1 pint) pudding basins, greased
❀ Oven temperature: 160°C (325°F/Gas Mark 3); alternatively, steam the pudding in a
   saucepan
❀ Steaming time: 2 hours

Sift the flour, baking powder and spice into a bowl. Mix in the breadcrumbs, suet, fruit
and walnuts. In a measuring jug, combine the apple juice, lemon juice, rind and sugar.

Combine the wet and dry mixtures, beat well for one minute. Divide into the
prepared pudding basins. Cover the basins with greaseproof paper. Steam them in the
oven for approximately 2 hours.

Store the puddings in the refrigerator. Before serving, steam them for about one
hour.

Plum Pudding

Vegan

This is a vegetarian adaptation of a very old recipe. In her famous *Book of Household Management*, Mrs. Beeton describes it as "An excellent plum pudding made without eggs." However, as with most plum puddings, this one does not contain any plums at all.

200 g (7 oz/1½ cups) plain flour
150 g (5 oz/1 cup) currants
150 g (5 oz/1 cup) raisins
50 g (2 oz/¼ cup) chopped mixed peel
100 g (3½ oz/½ cup) grated vegetable suet or fat
100 g (3½ oz/½ cup) sugar
100 g (3½ oz/½ cup) mashed boiled carrots
100 g (3½ oz/½ cup) mashed boiled potatoes
1 tablespoon molasses

❁ One-step method
❁ Cake tin: one 1 litre (2 pint) pudding basin, greased
❁ Oven temperature: 180°C (350°F/Gas Mark 4); alternatively, steam the pudding in a saucepan
❁ Steaming time: about 2 hours

Mix the flour, currants, raisins, mixed peel, suet and sugar together. Stir in the mashed carrots and potatoes. Add the molasses but no other liquid. Mix well and spoon the mixture into the basin. Steam in a saucepan or in the oven until well risen, about 2 hours.

Serve with custard, evaporated milk or Greek-style yoghurt.

SMALL CAKES

*I*n practice, all mixtures for sponge cakes can be baked in cupcake cases. (See, for example, the recipe for Honey Sponge on p. 52.) However, there are recipes which only work for small cakes, such as Muffins and Rock Cakes.

Not all small cakes are baked; some are deep-fried, such as Gulab Jamuns from India and traditional Doughnuts. Some are steamed, such as Cassava Cakes from Southeast Asia, and some are grilled – Pancakes and Scotch Potato Cakes, for example.

Rock Cakes

VEGAN

Despite their name, Rock Cakes are not supposed to be hard. They are so called because they look like miniature rocks.

❀ Ingredients for 12 cakes:
200 g (7 oz/1½ cups) wholemeal flour
2 teaspoons baking powder
100 g (3½ oz/½ cup) muscovado sugar
30 g (1 oz/2 tablespoons) butter or vegetable margarine
150 ml (5 fl oz/⅔ cup) yoghurt or soya yoghurt
100 g (3½ oz/¾ cup) raisins
50 g (2 oz/2 tablespoons) chopped mixed peel
2 tablespoons milk or soya milk (for brushing)

❀ Rub-in method
❀ Cake tin: one large rectangular tin or baking sheet, greased
❀ Oven temperature: 180°C (350°F/Gas Mark 4)
❀ Baking time: 15 minutes

Sift together the flour, baking powder and sugar. Rub in the butter until the mixture resembles fine breadcrumbs. Make a well in the centre and add the yoghurt, a little at a time. Mix thoroughly until well blended. Mix in the raisins and peel.

Spoon the mixture onto the prepared tin, one spoonful at a time, forming the "rocks". Make sure to leave plenty of room between the cakes. Brush the tops with a little milk. Bake for 15 minutes. Allow to cool before serving.

Scones

Vegan

❁ Ingredients for 12 scones:
200 g (7 oz/1½ cups) plain or wholemeal flour
2 teaspoons baking powder
50 g (2 oz/¼ cup) caster sugar
½ teaspoon salt
25 g (1 oz/2 tablespoons) cold butter or vegetable margarine
150 ml (5 fl oz/⅔ cup) yoghurt or soya yoghurt
2 tablespoons milk or soya milk (for brushing)

❁ Rub-in method
❁ Cake tin: one large rectangular tin or baking sheet, greased
❁ Oven temperature: 190°C (375°F/Gas Mark 5)
❁ Baking time: 12–15 minutes

In a bowl, mix the flour, baking powder, salt and sugar. Rub in the butter until the mixture resembles fine breadcrumbs. Add the yoghurt and mix with your fingers just until the ingredients are combined. Gently form the pastry into a shape about 2 cm (¾") thick. Cut into 4 cm (1¾") circles. Place the circles on the tin and brush the tops with a little milk. Bake for 12 to 15 minutes. Allow to cool for a few minutes before cutting open. Serve warm with butter or jam.

❁ Variations:
Spicy: add ½ teaspoon ginger and ½ teaspoon mixed spice.
Cheese: omit the sugar; add 2 tablespoons grated vegetarian cheese.
Coconut: add 2 tablespoons grated coconut.
Currant: add 4 tablespoons currants.

Gulab Jamuns

500 ml (2 pint/4 cups) water
400 g (14 oz/2 cups) any unrefined sugar
1 tablespoon rosewater
200 g (7 oz/1½ cups) whole milk powder
50 g (2 oz /¼ cup) plain flour
1 tablespoon soft butter
½ teaspoon bicarbonate of soda
100 ml (3½ fl oz/½ cup) fresh milk
ghee (clarified butter) or good quality vegetable oil for deep-frying

In a saucepan, make a syrup by mixing the water and the sugar and boiling for 3 minutes. Add the rosewater and remove from the heat.

In a mixing bowl, mix the milk powder, flour, butter, bicarbonate of soda and enough fresh milk to make a firm dough. Form little balls of dough, 2 cm (¾") in diameter, and put aside.

Heat the ghee or oil in a large wok or deep saucepan. Fry the balls of dough a few at a time over low heat until golden brown. Drain on paper towels and place into the syrup. Leave them for at least 4 hours. Serve cold.

Muffins

Vegan

❋ Ingredients for 12:
200 g (7 oz/1½ cups) plain or wholemeal flour
4 teaspoons baking powder
1 teaspoon ground cinnamon (optional)
25 g (1 oz/¼ cup) carob powder
100 g (3½ oz/½ cup) honey or molasses
50 ml (2 fl oz/3 tablespoons) sunflower oil
200 ml (7 fl oz/½ cup) milk or soya milk

❋ Dry and wet method
❋ Cake tins: 12 muffin tins, greased and floured, or line with 12 muffin paper cases
❋ Oven temperature: 180°C (350°F/Gas Mark 4)
❋ Baking time: 15–20 minutes

In a mixing bowl, sift the flour, baking powder, cinnamon and carob powder. In a jug, mix the honey, oil and milk. Combine the two mixtures and beat with a spoon for 2 minutes.

Spoon the mixture into the prepared tins and bake for 15 to 20 minutes. Allow to cool for 5 minutes before turning out.

Cassava Cakes

VEGAN

❀ Ingredients for 8 cakes:
500 g (1 lb/2 cups) grated yam or manioc
100 g (3½ oz/1 cup) grated coconut
100 g (3½ oz/½ cup) caster sugar
1 large saucepan of boiling water

❀ Steaming time: 1 hour

Peel the yam under running water and grate it. In a mixing bowl, mix the grated yam, coconut and sugar. Divide the mixture into eight parts and wrap each one in a square of foil.

Place the cakes in a colander and place the colander over the boiling water, but make sure that the parcels do not touch the water. Cook for approximately 1 hour. Add more boiling water as the level lowers.

Serve cold with fresh fruit such as pineapple, mango, peach, passion fruit, orange, banana, etc.

Maids of Honour

❁ Ingredients for 12:
600 ml (1 pint/2½ cups) milk
1 teaspoon vegetable rennet
250 g (9 oz/½ quantity) Easy Puff Pastry (see p. 174)
1 tablespoon cornflour
1 tablespoon water
15 g (½ oz/1 tablespoon) butter
50 g (2 oz/¼ cup) caster sugar

❁ One-step method
❁ Cake tins: 12 patty or fairy cake tins, greased
❁ Oven temperature: 200°C (400°F/Gas Mark 6)
❁ Baking time: 30 minutes

Heat the milk till just warm to the finger. Remove from the heat and stir in the vegetable rennet. Leave for 2 hours or until set. Pour the curds into a muslin bag and leave to drain overnight. Next day, chill until firm, about 2 hours.

Roll out the pastry thinly and cut twelve 7½ cm (3") rounds. Line the tins with the pastry rounds and prick them with a fork. Dissolve the cornflour in the water. Melt the butter over low heat. Stir in the sugar, drained curd and dissolved cornflour. Divide the mixture into the tins and bake for 30 minutes. They should rise while in the oven and fall again once removed. Serve warm.

Lebkuchen

VEGAN

Also called Pfefferkuchen, these cakes come from Germany and are served on special occasions.

150 g (5 oz/1¼ cups) plain flour
½ teaspoon allspice
½ teaspoon ground aniseed
1 teaspoon baking powder
50 g (2 oz/¼ cup) chopped almonds
50 g (2 oz/¼ cup) raisins
25 g (1 oz/2 tablespoons) mixed chopped peel
100 g (3½ oz/½ cup) butter or vegetable margarine
100 g (3½ oz/½ cup) honey or golden syrup

❀ Melting method
❀ Cake tin: one large rectangular tin or baking sheet, greased
❀ Oven temperature: 160°C (325°F/Gas Mark 3)
❀ Baking time: 15 minutes

Sift the flour, spices and baking powder into a bowl. Toss in the almonds, raisins and peel. In a saucepan, melt the butter, remove from the heat and mix in the honey. Add this mixture to the dry one and mix well.

Leave the dough to rest for 6 hours or overnight. Form little round cakes and place them carefully on the greased baking tray. Bake for 15 minutes. When cool, toss them in icing sugar or dip them in melted carob pieces or Mock Chocolate. Store the cakes in an airtight tin.

Pancakes

VEGAN

50 g (2 oz/¼ cup) melted butter or vegetable margarine
50 g (2 oz/⅓ cup) plain flour
25 g (1 oz/¼ cup) cornflour
a pinch of salt (optional)
½ teaspoon baking powder
250 ml (8 fl oz/1 cup) milk or soya milk

❀ One-step method
❀ Cooking time: approx. 5 minutes each side on a griddle, frying pan or skillet

Melt the butter over low heat. Allow to cool slightly. In the meantime, sift the flour, cornflour, salt and baking powder into a bowl. Stir in the milk and cooled butter and whisk vigorously for 1 minute.

For large pancakes such as French crêpes: drop 2 tablespoons of mixture onto a hot griddle, covering the base thinly. Cook until the underside is golden. Turn over and cook the other side. Repeat until all the batter has been used.

For Scotch pancakes: drop 1 tablespoon of batter per pancake. You can cook 3 or 4 pancakes at a time. Cook until the underside is golden, turn over and cook the other side. Serve warm with honey and lemon juice or maple syrup.

Gluten-free Carob Cakes

VEGAN

100 g (3½ oz/¾ cup) buckwheat flour or quinoa flour
50 g (2 oz/½ cup) potato flour
25 g (1 oz/¼ cup) carob powder
1 teaspoon bicarbonate of soda
100 ml (3½ fl oz/½ cup) cold milk or fruit juice
4 tablespoons sunflower oil
50 g (2 oz/¼ cup) muscovado sugar
½ teaspoon vanilla essence
the juice of 1 lemon

❀ Dry and wet method
❀ Cake tins: 12 fairy cake cases
❀ Oven temperature: 180°C (350°F/Gas Mark 4)
❀ Baking time: 15 minutes

Sift flours, carob and bicarbonate of soda. In a measuring jug, measure the milk or juice and oil. Dissolve the sugar in it. Add the vanilla and lemon juice. Pour this mixture over the dry mixture and beat for one minute.

Spoon the mixture into the cases. Bake for 15 minutes. Let cool completely before icing with Orange Icing or Lemon Icing.

Doughnuts

VEGAN

❀ Ingredients for 12:
250 ml (8 fl oz/1 cup) warm milk or soya milk
15 g (½ oz) fresh yeast
500 g (1 lb/3¾ cups) strong white flour
50 g (2 oz/¼ cup) butter or vegetable margarine
1 teaspoon salt
50 g (2 oz/¼ cup) sugar
ghee (clarified butter) or good quality vegetable oil for deep-frying
caster sugar for dredging

❀ Bread-making method
❀ Frying time: 10 minutes
❀ Rising time: 1 hour
❀ Proving time: 30–40 minutes

Heat the milk till just warm to the finger. Add the yeast and dissolve it by crumbling it between your fingertips. Mix in 1 tablespoon flour. Cover with a tea towel and leave for 10 minutes.

In a mixing bowl, cut the butter into the flour and rub it in until the mixture resembles fine breadcrumbs. Mix in the salt and sugar. Make a well in the centre and pour in the yeast mixture. Mix with your fingers, turn the dough onto a floured surface and knead for 10 minutes. Place the dough in an oiled bowl. Cover and leave to rise for about 1 hour.

Knead the dough again for 1 to 2 minutes, divide into 12 balls and place them on a floured surface. Cover with a cloth and leave to rise for 30 to 40 minutes, until about doubled in size. Fry a few at a time in deep, hot ghee or vegetable oil until golden. When the undersides are cooked, turn them gently and cook the other side. Drain on paper towels and toss in caster sugar.

Variations:
❀ Jam Doughnuts: When the doughnuts are cool, make a little incision in each and "inject" 2 teaspoons strawberry or raspberry jam.
❀ Custard Doughnuts: When the doughnuts are cool, make a slit on one side and fill the centres with Confectioner's Custard (Crème Pâtisserie).
❀ Chocolate Doughnuts: Spread the tops of the doughnuts with melted carob drops or pieces. Sprinkle with carob vermicelli or strands of "hundreds and thousands".
❀ Ring Doughnuts: Roll out risen dough to about 1½ cm (½") in thickness and cut into 5 cm (2") rings. Prove and deep-fry as above.

Scotch Potato Cakes

VEGAN

200 g (½ lb/2 cups) mashed potatoes
50 g (2 oz/½ cup) potato flour
15 g (½ oz/1 tablespoon) vegetable margarine or butter
¼ teaspoon salt

❀ One-step method
❀ Baking time: 15–20 minutes

Mix all the ingredients. Form little cakes between the palms of the hands and bake 3 minutes each side on a hot griddle or heavy frying pan. Serve hot, spread with butter.

SAVOURY CAKES

These recipes are wonderful for picnics, lunch boxes and buffets. They can also be used as a main dish if served with baked potatoes, salads or steamed vegetables.

Spinach Roll

Vegan

300 ml (10 fl oz/1¼ cups) warm milk or soya milk
15 g (½ oz) fresh yeast
500 g (1 lb 2 oz/4 cups) strong bread flour (white or wholemeal, or equal amounts of both)
1 teaspoon salt
60 ml (2 fl oz/¼ cup) sunflower oil

❁ Filling:
250 g (½ lb/2 cups) spinach
1 tablespoon butter or vegetable margarine
a pinch of salt
a pinch of ground black pepper
½ teaspoon ground nutmeg
200 g (7 oz/1 cup) grated Cheddar cheese or firm tofu

❁ Bread-making method
❁ Rising and proving time: 90 minutes
❁ Cake tin: a large rectangular tin or baking sheet, greased
❁ Oven temperature: 220°C (425°F/Gas Mark 7) for 15 minutes and 180°C (350°F/ Gas Mark 4) for 20–25 minutes
❁ Baking time: 35–40 minutes

Heat the milk till just warm to the finger. Remove from the heat and stir in the yeast, crumbling it into the milk with your fingers. Mix in one heaped tablespoon flour. Cover with a tea towel and leave for 10 minutes.

In a mixing bowl, mix the remaining flour, salt and oil. Stir in the milk and yeast mixture. Knead for 5 minutes, form into a ball and place in an oiled bowl. Cover and leave to rise for 1 hour.

In the meantime, wash and drain the spinach. In a saucepan, melt the butter, add the spinach and cook it in the water clinging to its leaves. Add salt, pepper and nutmeg. When cooked, remove from the heat and drain. Reserve any cooking liquid for soups or other dishes.

Roll out the pastry into an oblong about 30 × 40 cm (12" × 14"). Spread the spinach on top and cover with grated cheese. Roll up carefully and seal all the edges.

Place the roll on the prepared cake tin and leave it to prove for 30 minutes. Bake at 220°C (425°F/Gas Mark 7) for 15 minutes. Lower the heat to 180°C (350°F/Gas Mark 4) and bake for another 20 to 25 minutes. Serve hot.

Vegetable Cake

VEGAN

300 g (10 oz/2½ cups) flour
½ teaspoon ground black pepper
6 teaspoons baking powder
1 teaspoon salt
100 ml (3½ fl oz/½ cup) sunflower oil
2 tablespoons grated cheese or tofu
300 ml (10 fl oz/1¼ cups) milk or soya milk
250 g (8 oz/1½ cups) chopped French beans, parboiled
2 carrots, chopped and parboiled
100 g (3½ oz/½ cup) chopped olives
1 tablespoon chopped parsley

❀ One-step method
❀ Cake tin: one 1 kg (2 lb) loaf tin or one 20 cm (8") ring mould, greased and floured
❀ Oven temperature: 180°C (350°F/Gas Mark 4)
❀ Baking time: 40–45 minutes

In a bowl, mix the flour, black pepper, baking powder and salt. Add the oil, cheese and milk, and mix. Stir in the cooled cooked vegetables, the olives and parsley. Beat for 1 minute with a spoon.

Spoon into the prepared cake tin. Bake for 40 to 45 minutes. Check if the centre of the cake is dry. If it is not, leave in the oven for another 5 minutes. Let the cake cool for 10 minutes and then turn out.

This savoury cake can be served hot or cold. To reheat, wrap it in greaseproof paper and heat it in a warm oven for 10 to 15 minutes.

Layered Vegetable Cake

VEGAN

200 g (7 oz/1½ cups) flour
4 teaspoons baking powder
300 ml (10 fl oz/1¼ cups) milk or soya milk
50 ml (2 fl oz/¼ cup) sunflower oil
50 g (2 oz/½ cup) cornflour
50 g (2 oz/4 tablespoons) grated cheddar cheese (optional)
1 teaspoon salt

✻ Filling: 1 tablespoon olive oil
2 ripe tomatoes, chopped
300 g (10 oz/2 cups) chopped mixed vegetables: carrots, French beans, sweet corn,
    peas, peppers, etc.
a pinch of salt, a pinch of ground black pepper
1 tablespoon chopped parsley

✻ One-step method
✻ Cake tin: one 18 × 25 cm (7" × 10") tin, for a deep cake, greased and floured, or one
    20 × 30 cm (8" × 12") for a shallower cake
✻ Oven temperature: 180°C (350°F/Gas Mark 4)
✻ Baking time: 35–40 minutes

First prepare the filling: In a saucepan, heat the oil and sauté the vegetables over low
heat for a few minutes. Add the salt, pepper and parsley. Remove from the heat and set
aside.

For the cake mixture, combine all the ingredients in a large bowl. Beat for 2 minutes
with a wire whisk. Spread half of the batter onto the prepared tin. Spread with the
vegetable filling and cover with the rest of the batter. Bake for 35 to 40 minutes. Serve
hot or cold.

Pizza Roll

300 ml (10 fl oz/1¼ cups) lukewarm water
15 g (½ oz) fresh yeast
500 g (1 lb 2 oz/4 cups) strong bread flour (white or wholemeal, or equal amounts of
    both)
1 teaspoon salt
1 teaspoon oregano
3 tablespoons olive oil

❀ Filling:
5 ripe tomatoes, peeled and chopped
1 tablespoon olive oil
1 teaspoon oregano
1 teaspoon basil
a pinch of salt
½ teaspoon ground black pepper
200 g (7 oz/1 cup) grated or chopped mozzarella cheese

❀ Bread-making method
❀ Rising and proving time: 90 minutes
❀ Cake tin: one large rectangular tin or baking sheet, greased
❀ Oven temperature: 220°C (425°F/Gas Mark 7) for 15 minutes and 180°C (350° F/Gas
    Mark 4) for 20–25 minutes
❀ Baking time: 35–40 minutes

Heat the water till just warm to the finger. Add the yeast and dissolve it in the water. Stir
in 1 heaped tablespoon flour. Cover with a tea towel and leave for 10 minutes.
    In a mixing bowl, mix the flour, salt, oregano and oil. Stir in the yeast mixture.
Knead for 5 minutes, form into a ball and place in an oiled bowl. Cover and leave to rise
for about 1 hour.

In the meantime, wash, peel and chop the tomatoes. In a saucepan, heat the oil and add the herbs, salt and pepper. Stir in the tomatoes and cook them over medium heat for 2 or 3 minutes. Leave to cool.

Roll out the pastry into an oblong about 30 × 40 cm (12" × 14"). Spread the tomatoes on top and cover with grated mozzarella, reserving 1 tablespoon for the top. Roll up carefully and seal all the edges. Sprinkle with the rest of the mozzarella.

Place the roll on the prepared cake tin and leave it to prove for 30 minutes. Bake at 220°C (425°F/Gas Mark 7) for 15 minutes, then lower the heat to 180°C (350°F/Gas Mark 4) and bake for another 20 to 25 minutes. Serve hot.

Celery Bread

VEGAN

300 g (10 oz/2½ cups) plain flour
5 teaspoons baking powder
1 teaspoon salt
50 g (2 oz/¼ cup) butter or vegetable margarine
200 ml (7 fl oz/¾ cup) milk or soya milk
100 g (3½ oz/¾ cup) chopped celery, including leaves
150 g (5 oz/¾ cup) grated cheddar cheese or tofu

❈ Rub-in method
❈ Cake tin: one ½ kg/1 lb loaf tin, greased and floured
❈ Oven temperature: 190°C/375°F/Gas Mark 5
❈ Baking time: 35–40 minutes

Sift the flour, baking powder and salt into a mixing bowl. Chop the cold butter or margarine and rub into the flour until the mixture resembles fine breadcrumbs.

Stir in the milk. Add the celery and the cheese, mixing with your fingertips for 2 or 3 minutes. Shape into a loaf and place in the prepared tin.

Bake for 35 minutes or until well risen and golden. Allow to cool for 10 minutes before turning out. Serve sliced and buttered.

Christmas Chestnut Roll

VEGAN

2 tablespoons butter or vegetable margarine
2 tablespoons water
1 tablespoon cornflour
100 g (3½ oz/¾ cup) plain flour
2 teaspoons baking powder
100 ml (3½ fl oz/½ cup) milk or soya milk
½ teaspoon salt
1 teaspoon basil
1 teaspoon chopped parsley

✳ Filling and topping:
1 tablespoon olive oil
1 teaspoon dried basil
500 g (1 lb/1½ cups) chestnut purée
½ teaspoon salt
½ teaspoon ground black pepper

✳ One-step method
✳ Cake tins: 1 Swiss roll tin or one 18 × 25 cm (7" × 10") rectangular tin, greased and floured
✳ Oven temperature: 180°C (350°F/Gas Mark 4)
✳ Baking time: 15–20 minutes

For the cake batter, melt the butter and stir in the water and cornflour. Mix in the other ingredients. Spoon the mixture into the prepared tin and bake for 15 to 20 minutes, or until dry and golden.

Let the cake cool for 5 minutes. In the meantime, prepare the filling: In a saucepan, heat the oil and add the basil. Stir in the chestnut purée, salt and pepper.
Turn the cake out onto a slightly damp tea towel. Spread with half of the filling and roll

up tightly. Hold in place for a few minutes. Remove the tea towel.

Place the cake on a serving dish. Spread the other half of the filling on the "log" and make patterns with a fork, imitating bark. Decorate with sprigs of parsley or other fresh herbs. Serve hot with sautéed vegetables or a salad.

Tomato and Basil Cakes

VEGAN

4 tomatoes
1 tablespoon olive oil
300 g (10 oz/2½ cups) self-raising flour
2 teaspoons baking powder
½ teaspoon ground cayenne pepper
½ teaspoon salt
75 ml (3 fl oz/⅓ cup) sunflower oil
250 ml (8 fl oz/1 cup) milk or soya milk
3 tablespoons fresh, chopped basil or 2 teaspoons dry basil
100 g (3½ oz/½ cup) grated cheddar cheese or tofu

❉ One-step method
❉ Cake tins: 24 fairy cake tins, greased and floured
❉ Oven temperature: 180°C (350°F/Gas Mark 4)
❉ Baking time: 10–15 minutes

Place the tomatoes in a bowl of very hot water for a few minutes. Lift out with a
fork and peel. Cut in quarters, remove the seeds and chop. Heat the olive oil, add the
tomatoes and shallow-fry for 2 or 3 minutes.

Sift the flour, baking powder, pepper and salt into a mixing bowl. Stir in the
sunflower oil and milk. Add the tomatoes, the basil and half of the cheese. Beat with
a spoon for a minute.

Spoon the mixture into the prepared tins. Sprinkle the remaining cheese on top
of the cakes. Bake for 10 to 15 minutes or until springy and golden. Serve hot or cold.

EVERYDAY ICINGS AND FILLINGS

These recipes are both delicious and nutritious and can be used in everyday cooking.

Fruit Filling
VEGAN

2 cups chopped fresh fruit: apples, bananas, pears, peaches, pineapple, apricots,
    or a mixture
1 tablespoon lemon juice
1 tablespoon muscovado sugar

Peel and chop the fruit. Cook over low heat until soft. Add lemon juice and sugar and
mash with a fork or potato masher. Leave to cool slightly before spreading on the cake.

Fruit and Nut Filling 1
VEGAN

200 g (7 oz/1¼ cups) dried fruit: raisins, sultanas, currants, dates, figs, bananas, etc.,
    or a mixture
100 g (3½ oz/½ cup) hazelnuts, walnuts, cashews or brazils

Soak the fruit in hot water for half an hour. Drain and blend or mash. Toast the nuts in
a low oven or under the grill for a few minutes. Grind in a grinder or place them on a
tea towel, close like a bag and roll a rolling pin over them. Combine the fruit and nuts
and spread on the cake.

Fruit and Nut Filling 2
VEGAN

100 g (3½ oz/½ cup) dates
2 tablespoons peanut butter
6 tablespoons honey or golden syrup
50 g (2 oz/½ cup) carob powder
50 g (2 oz/2 tablespoons) sesame seeds, ground

50 g (2 oz/4 tablespoons) sunflower seeds, ground
50 g (2 oz/½ cup) grated coconut

Soak the dates in hot water for an hour. Drain and blend or mash. Heat the peanut butter and honey, but do not boil. Add the carob and mix well. Remove from the heat and mix in all the other ingredients. Use while still warm.

Sweetcorn Icing

200 g (7 oz/1 cup) sweetcorn
50 g (2 oz/¼ cup) caster sugar
15 g (½ oz/2 tablespoons) cornflour
1 tablespoon butter or vegetable margarine
200 ml (7 fl oz/¾ cup) milk or soya milk

Cook the sweetcorn until soft. Blend until liquid. Mix with all the other ingredients and cook over low heat until thickened, stirring constantly with a spoon.

Ricotta Icing

25 g (1 oz/2 tablespoons) soft butter or vegetable margarine
50 g (2 oz/¼ cup) caster sugar
250 g (½ lb/1¼ cups) fresh ricotta cheese
a few drops vanilla essence or lemon juice

Beat the butter with the sugar until light and creamy. Beat in the ricotta a little at a time. Add the vanilla essence or lemon juice. Add 1 teaspoon grated lemon or lime rind if you want to give it extra zest.

Mixed Nut Filling

VEGAN

200 g (7 oz/1 cup) mixed nuts (hazelnuts, walnuts, pecans, cashews, almonds, pistachios or brazils)
1 tablespoon butter or margarine
2 tablespoons milk or soya milk
1 tablespoon muscovado sugar

Toast the nuts in a warm oven. When cool, grind in a grinder or blender, or place them on a tea towel, close like a bag and roll a rolling pin over them.

In a saucepan, melt the butter and add the milk. Stir in the nuts, remove from the heat and add the sugar. Beat with a spoon until the mixture thickens.

Aduki Bean Filling

VEGAN

100 g (3½ oz/½ cup) aduki beans
100 g (3½ oz/½ cup) muscovado or unrefined granulated sugar
1 teaspoon vanilla essence

Soak the beans overnight. Drain them and place in a saucepan half-filled with water. Boil vigorously for 10 minutes without the lid. Cover the saucepan, lower the heat and cook for approximately 1 to 1½ hours, or until very soft. Add more boiling water if necessary.

Allow to cool. Mash the beans with a potato masher or in a food processor. Add the sugar and the vanilla. Beat until light and fluffy.

Mixed Nut Filling

See-through Icing

Vegan

200 ml (7 fl oz/¾ cup) orange juice
15 g (½ oz/1 tablespoon) sugar
2 teaspoons arrowroot

Mix all ingredients in a saucepan and cook over low heat, stirring constantly, until thickened. Do not let it boil. Cool for 2 or 3 minutes and spread on the cake.

Crème Pâtisserie, or Confectioner's Custard

2 tablespoons cornflour
300 ml (½ pint/1¼ cups) milk or soya milk
50 g (2 oz/¼ cup) unsalted butter or vegetable margarine
50 g (2 oz/¼ cup) sugar
½ teaspoon vanilla essence

In a cup, mix the cornflour in 3 tablespoons cold milk. Place the rest of the milk in a saucepan and boil over low heat. Add the butter and let it melt. Mix in the sugar. Add the cornflour diluted in cold milk and stir until the mixture thickens. Remove from the heat and stir in the vanilla. Leave to cool for a few minutes before spreading on the cake.

✴ Variation: Chocolate Crème: add 1 tablespoon sifted carob powder to the cornflour and milk mixture.

Soft Cheese Icing

200 g (7 oz/¾ cup) low- or medium-fat soft cheese
50 ml (2 fl oz/¼ cup) Greek-style or other creamy yoghurt
50 g (2 oz/¼ cup) caster sugar
½ teaspoon vanilla essence or 1 teaspoon lemon juice

Beat the cheese with the yoghurt and sugar until light and creamy. Add the vanilla
essence or lemon juice. Add 1 teaspoon grated lemon or lime rind if you want to give it
extra zest.

Tofu Icing

25 g (1 oz/2 tablespoons) vegetable margarine
50 g (2 oz/2 tablespoons) muscovado sugar, sifted
200 g (7 oz/1 cup) diced tofu
a few drops of vanilla essence or lemon juice

Beat the margarine with the sugar until light and creamy. Beat in the tofu a little at a
time. Add the vanilla essence or lemon juice. Add 1 teaspoon grated lemon or lime rind
if you want to give it extra zest.

ICINGS AND FILLINGS FOR SPECIAL OCCASIONS

These icings and fillings are rich and sweet, for those special cakes.

Butter Icing
Vegan

100 g (3½ oz/½ cup) unsalted butter or vegetable margarine
250 g (8 oz/1 cup) icing sugar, sifted
a few drops vanilla essence
50 ml (2 fl oz/3 tablespoons) milk or soya milk

Cream the butter or margarine until soft. Beat in the sugar a little at a time, adding the vanilla essence and enough milk to give a fairly firm but spreading consistency.

Butter Icing can be coloured with natural food colouring. Add a few drops of colouring with the vanilla essence.

Variations:
❊ Carob: add 1 tablespoon sifted carob powder to the sugar.
❊ Coconut: substitute coconut milk for the milk, or add 2 tablespoons grated coconut.
❊ Coffee: dissolve 1 tablespoon instant barley coffee into 1 tablespoon hot water and 2 tablespoons milk or soya milk. Omit the milk in the recipe.
❊ Orange: substitute orange juice for the milk. Add 1 tablespoon grated orange rind. Omit the vanilla.
❊ Lemon: substitute lemon juice for the milk. Add 1 tablespoon grated orange rind. Omit the vanilla.

Chantilly Cream

250 ml (8 fl oz/1 cup) whipping or double cream
1 tablespoon icing sugar
½ teaspoon vanilla essence

The secret of a good Chantilly Cream is to beat it when the ingredients are ice cold, using utensils which are also very cold. Therefore, before you start, place the mixing bowl, whisk and the cream itself in the refrigerator for at least half an hour. Add the sugar and vanilla when the cream begins to thicken.

Beat until the cream is thick and stands in peaks. If the cream starts to separate, it is because you have whisked it too much. Fold in a tablespoonful of cold milk and mix slowly and carefully until the cream is smooth. If you are preparing more than one quantity, beat only 1 cup of cream at a time so as not to let it become warm.

If you are using an electric mixer, start with low speed so as to incorporate as much air as possible. As the cream begins to thicken, increase the speed.

Ganache 1

VEGAN

250 ml (8 fl oz/1 cup) whipping cream or soya cream
100 g (3½ oz/½ cup) carob pieces or chopped Mock Chocolate

Place the cream in a saucepan and heat gently. When it begins to boil, stir in the carob pieces. Remove from the heat and stir gently until all the carob has melted into the cream. Use immediately.

Ganache 2

100 g (3½ oz/½ cup) carob pieces or chopped Mock Chocolate
250 ml (8 fl oz/1 cup) whipping cream

Place the carob in a dry dish and melt it over a saucepan of hot water. In a mixing bowl, whip the cream until light and fluffy. Fold in the melted carob. Mix carefully until well blended. Use immediately.

Vegan Chantilly Cream

300 ml (10 fl oz/1¼ cups) water
100 g (3½ oz/4 tablespoons) powdered soya milk
1 teaspoon agar-agar or another vegetable gelatine
50 g (2 oz/¼ cup) vegetable margarine
1 tablespoon icing sugar
½ teaspoon vanilla essence

Blend together the water and soya milk powder. Bring to a boil and add the agar-agar. If using a different jelly mixture, follow the manufacturer's instructions.

Beat the margarine and sugar. Add the milk mixture and vanilla and stir. Chill for a few hours, then beat again until stiff.

Carob Icing

15 g (½ oz/1 tablespoon) butter
15 g (½ oz/1 tablespoon) carob powder, sifted
400 g (14 oz/1½ cups) condensed milk
1 teaspoon vanilla essence

Melt the butter in a saucepan over low heat. Mix in the carob powder. Add the condensed milk and stir. Cook over low heat, stirring constantly with a spoon. When the mixture has thickened, remove from the heat. Add the vanilla and beat with a spoon for a couple of minutes. Leave to cool a little before using.

Carob Frosting

150 ml (5 fl oz/⅔ cup) whipping cream
5 drops vanilla essence
25 g (1 oz/¼ cup) carob powder
50 g (2 oz/2 tablespoons) icing sugar

Whip the cream and vanilla until it stands in peaks. In a separate bowl, sift the carob
and sugar and fold gently into the cream.

Lemon Icing
VEGAN

100 g (3½ oz/½ cup) icing sugar
the rind of 1 lemon, finely grated
15 g (½ oz/1 tablespoon) melted butter or vegetable margarine
1 tablespoon lemon juice
a little cream or vegan cream

Mix all ingredients together and cover the top of the cake with the icing. Let it dribble
down the sides. Allow to set for about 1 hour.

Orange Icing
VEGAN

100 g (3½ oz/½ cup) icing sugar
2 tablespoons orange juice
1 tablespoon orange rind, finely grated

Sift the sugar and add the orange juice and the grated rind. Mix well and spread over
the cake as soon as the cake is cool.

Peanut Butter Icing
VEGAN

50 g (2 oz/¼ cup) butter or vegetable margarine
50 g (2 oz/¼ cup) peanut butter
100 g (3½ oz/½ cup) soft brown sugar

Beat all ingredients together and spread while the cake is still warm. For a slab cake, spread the icing on top and place the cake under a hot grill. Leave until bubbly. Let the cake cool and then cut it into squares.

Shrikhand Icing

Shrikhand is a traditional Indian sweet. This version has been adapted to be used as a filling.

500 ml (1 pint/2 cups) yoghurt
50 g (2 oz/2 tablespoons) caster sugar
a few drops of vanilla essence or 1 tablespoon vanilla sugar
100 ml (3½ fl oz/½ cup) whipping cream, whipped

Line a colander or large strainer with cheesecloth and pour the yoghurt in it. Place over a bowl to collect the whey. Leave for 3 hours until the yoghurt is firm. In a bowl, beat the yoghurt, sugar and vanilla. Fold in the cream and spread on the cake.

Shrikhand Icing

Moulding Icing
VEGAN

200 g (7 oz/1 cup) icing sugar
50 g (2 oz/¼ cup) vegetable margarine
1 tablespoon liquid glucose or honey
natural food colourings (optional)
icing sugar for handling

Sift the icing sugar and mix in the margarine and liquid glucose. Add colourings if using. Press the mixture into a ball. Add more sugar if necessary. Mould into shapes: flowers, balls, etc. If you are not using it immediately, place the mixture in a freezer bag and reserve until required.

Marzipan–Almond Paste
VEGAN

2 tablespoons honey or liquid glucose
100 g (3½ oz/½ cup) caster sugar
200 g (7 oz/1½ cups) ground almonds or brazil nuts or a mixture
¼ teaspoon almond essence

Place the honey or glucose in a dish and warm it over a bowl of hot water. Mix in the sugar and almonds. Make a well in the centre and add the honey or glucose and essence. Mix with your fingertips till well blended. Knead for a minute. Avoid handling too much or the oil from the almonds will start to separate. If this happens, add a little more sugar and ground almonds.

Vegan Cream

150 ml (5 fl oz/⅔ cup) water
100 g (3½ oz/4 tablespoons) powdered soya milk
100 ml (3½ fl oz/½ cup) sunflower oil
½ teaspoon vanilla essence
1 teaspoon lemon juice
200 g (7 oz/1 cup) icing sugar, sifted

In a blender, mix the water and the powdered soya milk. Reduce speed and add the oil, vanilla, lemon juice and sugar. Chill for a few hours before spreading on the cake.

Mock Chocolate 1

VEGAN

For 250 g (8 oz) "chocolate":
100 g (3½ oz/½ cup) vegetable fat
50 g (2 oz/½ cup) carob powder, sifted
100 g (3½ oz/½ cup) icing sugar
1 teaspoon vanilla essence

In a saucepan, melt the fat. Do not overheat. In the meantime, place some greaseproof paper over a working surface. Remove the fat from the heat and mix in the carob, sugar and vanilla. Beat with a spoon for 1 minute.

Spread the mixture over the greaseproof paper to the desired thickness and smooth it with a spatula. Let it harden a little and then cut it. Refrigerate if you want to grate it.

Mock Chocolate 2
VEGAN

(For leaves and other decorations)
For 500 g (approx. 1 lb) "chocolate":
250 g (8 oz/2 cups) coconut or other hard vegetable fat
200 g (7 oz/1 cup) icing sugar
50 g (2 oz/½ cup) carob powder

Melt the fat in a saucepan over low heat. Allow to cool slightly. Add the sugar and carob powder and beat into a paste. On a sheet of baking parchment, draw leaves or other decorations with a pencil or food colouring pen, and turn the paper over.

Fill a paper or other disposable icing bag with the warm mock chocolate and cut a fine nozzle from the tip. Pipe the chocolate designs onto the baking parchment according to the drawings. Refrigerate until firm. Peel off carefully and use for decoration.

Store the remaining mock chocolate in small containers in the freezer and use as required. For grating, use straight out of the freezer. For icings and other decorations, place the container in a bowl of hot water and allow the paste to melt.

Glacé Icing
VEGAN

200 g (7 oz/1 cup) icing sugar
lemon juice

Sift the icing sugar into a bowl. Add enough lemon juice to give a fairly firm but spreading consistency. If the mixture is too thick, add more lemon juice a little at a time. If it is too thin add more sifted sugar.

Use immediately, as it dries out quickly. Spread a thin layer of icing over the cake when cold.

Fudge Icing

one 400 g (14 oz) tin condensed milk

Cover the tin, unopened, with water and cook for 1 hour in a pressure cooker or 2 hours in an ordinary saucepan, making sure to add more boiling water as the level drops. Let it cool completely before opening the tin. Do not attempt to open the tin while it is hot!

ADAPTING RECIPES

There are hundreds of ordinary cake recipes which can be adapted to a lacto-vegetarian or even vegan diet. The following section contains suggestions on how to choose and adapt recipes.

How to Choose Recipes

Read the recipe carefully and observe the flour-egg ratio. Choose recipes which use only 1 or 2 eggs for each 200 g (7 oz/1½ cups) flour.

How to Adapt Recipes

In cakes, eggs have two basic functions: to bind the ingredients and to leaven the cake.

The ideas below can help you adapt recipes which require few eggs. Use the dry and wet method when adapting recipes.

For sponge-type cakes:

Either:
Replace each egg with:
✿ 2 tablespoons milk
✿ ½ tablespoon of lemon juice
✿ ½ tablespoon of
bicarbonate of soda

Or:
Replace each egg with:
✿ 2 tablespoons milk
✿ ¼ teaspoon baking powder

Replace the butter with the same weight of
✿ sunflower oil

For fruit cakes:

Replace each egg with:
✿ 1 tablespoon cornflour
✿ 2 tablespoons water

What to Do When Everything's Gone Wrong

Cakes can go wrong even in the hands of the most experienced cooks and pâtissiers in the world. The secret is not to panic or despair. With a bit of patience nothing will be wasted; it can simply be transformed.

For example, if a cake crumbles, transform it into truffles. If a cake collapses, soak it in fruit juice and use it in a trifle. If the borders of the cake burn, cut them off, cover the rest in Confectioner's Custard or Carob Icing and give it a grand name (my favourite is "Chinese Pudding"). Nobody will know.

The possibilities are endless. If you don't want to use the cake immediately, seal it in a plastic bag and freeze it. Below are a few recipes to give you some ideas. All quantities are approximate.

If all else fails, put your cake in a plastic bag and go feed the ducks in the park.

Truffles

100 g (3½ oz/½ cup) carob or Mock Chocolate pieces
250 g (½ lb/2 cups) cake crumbs
2 tablespoons marmalade or apricot jam
1 or 2 tablespoons boiled milk
grated coconut or ground nuts for coating

Melt the carob over low heat. Put the cake crumbs in a bowl and make a well in the centre. Pour in the jam and melted carob. Stir with a fork, adding a little milk until all the ingredients are combined. Pinch off little balls, 2½ cm (1") in diameter. Roll them in grated coconut or ground nuts. If you wish, place them in little paper cases.

Trifle

enough pieces of cake to cover the bottom of a large heat-proof dish
200 ml (7 fl oz/¾ cup) fruit juice
250 ml (½ pint/1 cup) chopped fruit
250 ml (½ pint/1 cup) vegetarian jelly
½ quantity Crème Pâtisserie
½ quantity Chantilly Cream (optional)
"hundreds and thousands" for decoration

Place the pieces of cake in the dish and pour in the juice, allowing the cake to soak it up. Spread the fruit on top. Prepare the jelly according to the recipe on the packet and pour it over the fruit. Refrigerate until firm. Prepare the Crème Pâtisserie and pour it over the jelly. If you wish, decorate with Chantilly Cream. Sprinkle some "hundreds and thousands" on top. Serve chilled.

"Chinese Pudding"

whatever was left of a cake that burnt around the sides
2 tablespoons sugar
1 teaspoon vanilla essence
1 tablespoon carob powder
250 ml (½ pint/1 cup) boiled milk
1 quantity Crème Pâtisserie or Carob Icing

Dissolve the sugar, vanilla and carob in the milk while it is still hot. Place the cake in a dish and soak it in the milk mixture. Refrigerate. Prepare the icing and, when cold, spread it over the cake and chill. Decorate with "hundreds and thousands", grated coconut, ground nuts or whatever is available, and give it a grand name before serving.

INDEX

Regular page numbers refer to recipes, italic page numbers to photos.

Adapting Recipes   247
Aduki Bean Filling   230
Afternoon Tea Cake   107
Almond Cream Cake   162
Apfelstrudel   176, *177*
Apple and Banana Cake   140
Apple and Date Cake   116
Apple Cake   73
Apple Crumble Cake   114
Apple Pudding Cake   *184*, 185
Apple Ring   192
Apple Tea Bread   141
Apricot Cake   86, *87*
Ariette's Cake   35
arrowroot   20
baking powder, homemade   21
bicarbonate of soda   21
Banana and Cherry Cake   65
Banana and Walnut Cake   130
Banana Cake   64
Bara Brith   136
Barm Brack   138, *139*
Birthday Cake 1   32, 33
Birthday Cake 2   34
Black Forest Gâteau   156, *157*
Boiled Cake   133
Brazilian Cake   135
Brownies   62, *63*
bread-making method   26
buckwheat flour   20
butter   22
Butter Icing   236
Butterscotch Cake   66

cake mixing methods   25
cake tins   16, 27
Caramel Cake   37
Carob cakes
    Birthday Cake 2   34
    Black Forest Gâteau   156, *157*
    Brownies   62, *63*
    Cassata Cake   148
    Delicacy Cake   154
    Gluten-free Carob Cakes   209
    Mock Chocolate Cake   36
    Orange and Carob Squares   88
    Party Sponge   58, *59*
    Sachertorte   174
    Three-colour Cake   152
    Tiger Cake   *180*, 181
Carob Frosting   239
Carob Icing   238
carob powder   20
Carrot cakes
    Carrot Cake   91
    Old-fashioned Carrot Cake   92, *93*
    Spicy Carrot Cake   67
Cassata Cake   148
Cassava Cakes   205
caster sugar   22
Celery Bread   221
Chantilly Cream   236
Charioteer Cake   96
cheese   25
Cheesecake 1   149
Cheesecake 2   150, *151*
Cherry Cake   106

Cherry Loaf   115
"Chinese Pudding"   250
Chocolate (*see* Mock Chocolate)
Chocolate Doughnuts   211
Christmas Cake   120
Christmas Chestnut Roll   *222, 223*
Christmas Pudding 1   194
Christmas Pudding 2   195
Coconut Biscuits   168
Coconut Cake   68, 69
Coffee and Walnut Cake   38
condensed milk   23
Continental Sweet Loaf   132
cooling the cake   28
cornflour   19, 20
Crazy Carob Pudding   190
cream   23
creaming method   26
 Crème Pâtisserie, or Confectioner's
    Custard   232
Custard Doughnuts   211
Date and Walnut Cake   123
Date Squares   95
Delicacy Cake   154
Doughnuts   210
dried fruit and nuts   23
dry and wet method   25
Ekadashi Cakes
    Ekadashi Coconut Cake   183
    Ekadashi Fruit Cake   49
    Ekadashi Sponge   56
    Gluten-free Carob Cakes   209
    Scotch Potato Cakes   211
equipment   17
essences   24
fat   22
Fig Cake   111
flavourings   24
flour   19
Folar   102, *103*

freezing the cake   28
Fridge Cake   170
fructose   22
Fruit and Nut Filling 1   228
Fruit and Nut Filling 2   228
Fruit Filling   228
Fruit Gâteau   160, *161*
fruit juice   23
Fudge Icing   245
Ganache 1   237
Ganache 2   237
Gauranga Cake   158
Genoese Cake   45
Giant Jam Scone   82
Ginger cakes
    Ginger Sandwich Cake   46
    Ginger Squares   74, *75*
    Gingerbread   89
Glacé Icing   244
Gluten-free Carob Cakes   209
Gokula Cake   71
golden syrup   22
Granddad's Coconut Cake   146, *147*
Grandmother's Fridge Cake   168
Gulab Jamuns   202, *203*
Hazelnut Cake   137
honey   22
Honey cakes
    Honey Cake   118
    Honey Sponge   52
    Honey Squares   85
icing sugar   22
ingredients   19
Jam Doughnuts   211
Krishna Cake   72
Lancashire Parkin   79
Layered Vegetable Cake   218
Lebkuchen   207
Lemon Icing   239
Lemon Sponge   50

Lemon Tea Bread   142, *143*
Macrobiotic Cake   76
Maids of Honour   206
malt extract   22
Mango Gâteau   163
maple syrup   22
Marble Cake   117
margarine   23
Marzipan–Almond Paste   242
melting method   25
milk   23
Mille Sfoglie   172, *173*
Mixed Nut Filling   230
mixed spice, homemade   24
Mocha Cake   39
Mock Chocolate 1   243
Mock Chocolate 2   244
Mock Chocolate Cake   36
molasses   22
Molasses Fruit Cake   113
Moulding Icing   242
Muffins   204
muscovado sugar   22
Neapolitan Cake   166
Nrisimha Cake   159
Nutmeg Cake   110
nuts   23
oil   23
Old-fashioned Carrot Cake   92, *93*
one-step method   25
Orange and Carob Squares   88
Orange Icing   239
Orange Tea Bread   109
Oriental Cake   78
Pancakes   208
Panetone, Traditional   108
Party Sponge   58, *59*
Peach Squares   98, *99*
Peanut Butter Cake   104
Peanut Butter Icing   240

Pineapple Cake   155
Pizza Roll   219
Plum Pudding   196, *197*
Polenta Cake   70
Potato Cake   131
Potato Cakes, Scotch   211
potato flour   20
preparing the cake tin   27
preparing the oven   27
Prune and Brazil Nut Cake   122
Quick Fruit Cake   112
Quick Mix Sponge   54
Quick Yoghurt Sponge   43
Raisin Cake   83
Raspberry Gâteau   186, *187*
Rhubarb Cake   80, *81*
rice flour   20
Ricotta Icing   229
Ring Doughnuts   211
Rock Cakes   200
Royal Orange Cake   40, *41*
rub-in method   26
Sachertorte   174
Saffron Tea Bread   134
Scones   201
Scotch Potato Cakes   211
See-through Icing   232
Seed Cake   129
self-raising flour, homemade   19
Shepherd's Cake   42
Shrikhand Icing   240, *241*
sodium bicarbonate   21
Soft Cheese Icing   233
Spice Slice   90
Spicy Carrot Cake   67
Spinach Roll   214
Sponge Pudding   191
Stollen   126
storing the cake   28
Strawberry Gâteau   167

sugar   21
Sugarfree cakes
    Macrobiotic Cake   76
    Scotch Potato Cakes   211
    Sugarfree Sponge Cake   48
Sweetcorn Cake   77
Sweetcorn Icing   229
Sweetcorn Pudding   193
Swiss Roll   164, *165*
tahini   25
Tahini Squares   94
testing the cake   27
Three-colour Cake   152
Tiger Cake   *180*, 181
Tiramisù   181
tofu   25
Tofu Cake   84
Tofu Icing   233
Tomato and Basil Cakes   225
Traditional Panetone   108
Trifle   250
troubleshooting   29
Truffles   249
Tutti Frutti Cake   128
Upside Down Cake   182
Vegan Chantilly Cream   238
Vegan Cream   243

Vegan icings and fillings
    Aduki Bean Filling   230, *231*
    Butter Icing   236
    Crème Pâtisserie   232
    Fruit and Nut Filling 1   228
    Fruit and Nut Filling 2   228
    Fruit Filling   228
    Glacé Icing   244
    Lemon Icing   239
    Mixed Nut Filling   230
    Orange Icing   239
    Peanut Butter Icing   240
    See-through Icing   232
    Sweetcorn Icing   229
    Tofu Icing   233
    Vegan Chantilly Cream   238
    Vegan Cream   243
Vegan Sponge   47
Vegetable Cake   216, *217*
Velvet Cake   44
Walnut Cakes
    Date and Walnut Cake   123
    Walnut Cake   119
    Walnut Malt Loaf   105
whey   23
yeast   21
yoghurt   23

Great Vegetarian Dishes

The author is one of the Hare Krishna movement's most celebrated chefs. He knows that to enjoy spiritual rewards, and to be fit and healthy, you have to eat properly. With humour, patience and enthusiasm he has passed on his knowledge to a growing and appreciative audience worldwide. He has spent several years testing and refining the hundreds of international recipes presented in this very practical book.

192 pages, numerous colour photos, hardbound
ISBN 978-0-9593659-1-7

Cooking with Kurma

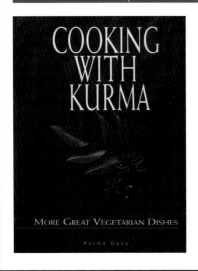

For the gourmet vegetarian, *Cooking with Kurma* can't be beat. Renowned throughout his Australian homeland as a master chef, Kurma has put together a useful cookbook that combines wit and mouth-watering recipes – more than 220 recipes from around the world.

256 pages, numerous colour photos, hardbound
ISBN 978-0-947259-17-4

Also available: an 11-part "Cooking with Kurma" video series that was broadcast on television throughout the U.S., England and the Middle East.

The Hare Krishna Book of Vegetarian Cooking

This book first explains utensils, the art of combining dishes in menu-planning, and preparing and eating an Indian meal. Then come 120 tested recipes, carefully chosen by an excellent cook in the Hare Krishna movement for their diversity and ease of preparation. Guaranteed to give you a whole new world of taste experience!

320 pages, 37 colour photographs, hardbound
ISBN 978-0-90267-07-4

The Higher Taste

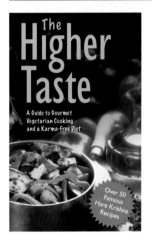

This small book is a great introduction to the philosophy and practice of vegetarianism, exploring the health and economic advantages as well as the ethical and spiritual considerations of a Krishna conscious approach to diet and nutrition. Containing over 50 recipes organized into nine delicious meals from around the world, *The Higher Taste* will teach you how to dramatically improve your life by changing the way you eat.

176 pages, 25 colour photographs, softbound
ISBN 978-1-84599-047-3

Available from www.blservices.com and www.krishna.com